PERSONAL FINANCE FOR TEENS

THE ULTIMATE GUIDE TO TRANSFORMING YOUR FINANCIAL GAME AT A YOUNG AGE - LEARN, EARN, AND INVEST TO GROW YOUR WEALTH

Emma Davis

Impact PUBLISHING

© Copyright Impact Publishing, LLC 2024 - All rights reserved. The content within this book may not be reproduced, duplicated, or transmitted without direct written permission from the author or the publisher.

Under no circumstances will any blame or legal responsibility be held against the publisher or author for any damages, reparation, or monetary loss due to the information contained within this book, either directly or indirectly. You are responsible for your own choices, actions, and results.

Legal Notice:

This book is copyright-protected and only for personal use. You cannot amend, distribute, sell, use, quote, or paraphrase any part of the content without the consent of the author or publisher.

Disclaimer Notice:

Please note that the information in this document is for educational and entertainment purposes only. All effort has been expended to present accurate, up-to-date, reliable, and complete information. No warranties of any kind are declared or implied. Readers acknowledge that the author is not engaging in the rendering of legal, financial, medical, or professional advice.

This book's content has been derived from various sources. Please consult a licensed professional before attempting any techniques outlined in this book.

By reading this document, the reader agrees that the author is under no circumstances responsible for any losses, direct or indirect, incurred as a result of using the information contained within this document, including, but not limited to, errors, omissions, or inaccuracies.

TABLE OF CONTENTS

Introduction .... *V*

Chapter1	Personal Finance Basics	1
Chapter2	All About Budgets	15
Chapter3	Master the Piggy Bank	28
Chapter4	Good Debt vs. Bad Debt	39
Chapter5	The Creditor's Quests	54
Chapter6	The Future Wealth	69
Chapter7	Exploring the Risk Factor	82
Chapter8	The Government's Share	96
Chapter9	Making It On Your Own	111
Chapter10	Financial Independence	123

Conclusion *131*

About The Author *137*

References *140*

This page has been intentionally left blank

INTRODUCTION

"Plan for the future because that is where you are going to spend the rest of your life."

— **Proverbio chino**

ARE YOU HAVING a hard time keeping up with your rich friends? Is the success of your favorite influencers making you toss and turn all night? Want a similar lifestyle?

If yes, then no worries, I have got you covered. As someone who was once in the same boat, I understand what you are going through, and now, I want to help you rescue yourself from the situation.

But first, let's get into a little story from my life, an event that changed how I viewed money.

One typical Friday morning, I found myself mindlessly scrolling through social media, idly admiring the luxurious and glamorous lives of my favorite influencers.

The constant stream of updates showcasing their possession of the latest gadgets, trendiest clothing, and jet-setting lifestyles served to fuel my feelings of envy and longing.

While scrolling, I received a notification on my screen. It was my friend inviting me to join them on a spontaneous weekend retreat. My heart raced with excitement at the thought of escaping from this boring everyday life, but then reality hit me hard. I checked my bank account, and my enthusiasm shattered into pieces. I realized I couldn't afford to go. Feeling disappointed, I switched off my phone and sat there, quiet, and dejected.

That was the time I realized that if I wanted to live a life of freedom and adventure, I must learn how to manage my finances. I was reminded of a quote by Natasha Munson:

"Money, like emotions, is something you must control to keep your life on the right track."

This deeply resonated with me and pushed me to start my journey. If I wanted to do things in life, I needed to be able to manage my money effectively.

Jojo Siwa, MrBeast, and Logan Paul are household names in the world of YouTube. Their immense wealth is notable because they flaunt it daily. Cars, houses, technology, basically everything in its grandeur. They make it all seem effortless and convenient. It might also impress you beyond compare and make you want a similar lifestyle. But, in almost all cases, the audience is unaware of the challenges they face. People on the receiving end of all the glamour do not know what happens behind the scenes. This is precisely what one needs to be mindful of before idealizing them. Struggle cannot be romanticized; the road to success is hard.

Let me decode their success stories for you.

JoJo Siwa, an American artist, vocalist, YouTuber, and media personality, started her journey to financial success early in life. She expanded her income streams by venturing into various business ventures, including music and even her line of products. Her story indeed teaches the world the importance of determination, creativity, and diversifying income sources to achieve financial success.

MrBeast, the YouTube sensation known for his entertaining videos and exhibit of generosity, has won the hearts of millions all over the world. Starting with a humble beginning, he monetized his interests into making content and then to a multi-million-dollar business. Despite the countless financial difficulties he encountered early life, he managed to become one of the wealthiest YouTubers in the world today. He has branched out from video making and now has his fast-food chain, MrBeast Burger, as well as Feastables, his line of chocolates. He revealed in a podcast that he reinvents every penny he makes. He is also known for philanthropy, as well as many business ventures. His incredible success can greatly be attributed to his genius-like business decisions.

Lastly, Logan Paul, is a notable internet influencer, professional wrestler, and entrepreneur. He has managed to come back from setbacks and controversies to build a successful brand for his name. He has extended his revenue streams by diving into different businesses, including stock, digital broadcasts, and businesses. His ability to adjust to changing conditions had a crucial impact on his financial achievement. Logan, through his determination, teaches us to never give up on dreams, no matter the obstacles we may face.

These inspiring stories of their struggle for success inspired me to begin my journey into the world of personal finance. A journey that led me to excel in financial empowerment and independence.

I'm not trying to brag about my expertise or how I figured it out. Nor am I some kind of financial expert who knows everything about personal finance, but I want to teach you the things I encountered and learned during my teenage years related to personal finance. I wish someone had taught me those skills when I was your age.

Financial independence is necessary if you want to be as successful as popular YouTubers. I know the road to achieving that is difficult. It is a process that requires a lot of effort and energy.

I also know being a teenager is not as easy as it seems. It's tough to juggle between academics, extracurricular activities, and a social life simultaneously. Also, managing limited finances takes a lot of effort, and the lack of guidance on personal finance can leave you feeling overwhelmed and unable to understand your financial responsibilities.

I understand the financial strain that comes from the pressure to continue to achieve the lavish lifestyles of influencers and celebrities portrayed on social media and other entertainment channels. I also cannot forget the FOMO, which does nothing but only adds to your financial stress.

In that desire, budgeting, saving, and investing are the last things that come to your mind. Believe me, the skills of personal finance are not just about managing and organizing your money but also about taking control of your future.

In today's fast-paced world, managing personal finances has become increasingly important. Money represents power, but its true strength lies in understanding its management. Money may come and go, but grasping how it works allows control and wealth building.

Fostering strong financial literacy and executing well-thought-out plans help achieve short- and long-term goals. Whether aiming for a luxurious lifestyle, buying a home, or pursuing higher education, effective financial planning remains crucial.

Taking charge of finances marks an empowering journey that demands discipline, commitment, and continuous learning. Building confidence by setting clear goals, crafting a budget, establishing an emergency fund, managing debt wisely, saving, investing for the future, and staying informed can lead to financial success.

According to Tamsen Butler (1974), "Many parents do not feel competent to teach personal finance, and it is not a subject taught in school."

You could be an individual who is just starting high school or preparing for college or someone who hasn't been taught about personal finance by your parents or in school. In either case, I know you might be a little scared to be financially savvy on your own. You can get started with this book, and it will lead you on the journey of financial freedom.

Personal finance management is an attitude and a mindset. The term 'personal finance' may sound boring to you, right? You may not even find this book relevant to your current situation, but I remember reading a quote from Robert Kiyosaki's book, Rich Dad Poor Dad. It says,

"Skills make you rich, not theories."

So, don't worry. This book does not merely lecture you on personal finance. Instead, it provides you with tried and tested strategies to help you learn how to create a budget that works for you, keep a check on your spending, and make brainy decisions about saving and investing.

Remember, it's not too late to start, and every step that takes you to the path to financial freedom begins with a solid plan. This book serves as your guide to help you embrace the journey toward financial freedom.

As Robert Kiyosaki said:

"Financial freedom is available to those who learn about it and work for it."

Financial freedom is achieved by learning about it and making an effort. It happens not by chance but through intentional actions and decisions.

Now that we're clear on one thing, let me tell you the distinction between the people who struggle with their financial condition and the financially stable people. This is an important difference to know before heading further into the journey.

The difference lies in key factors such as planning, resourcefulness, and literacy.

I. Planning

Financially stable individuals properly plan ways to use their money. Whether it's about saving for a car or a better lifestyle, they plan what they want to achieve from their money and reach their financial goals.

II. Resourcefulness

The people who know how to be resourceful become smart with their money use. Also, they find innovative ways to spend their money.

III. Literacy

Financially literate people are said to know about managing their money wisely. They understand the strategies of budgeting, saving, and investing. This is the reason they adopt smart financial decisions.

This book seeks to prepare teenagers like you with viable information on how to plan, be resourceful, and become financially literate as you work toward realizing your financial goals. The book also offers different tools and templates to enable you to plan your budgets, track your investing, and optimally allocate your stacks toward savings and investments.

This guide employs real-life examples that empower you to effectively understand complex budgetary concepts. The different exercises included in each chapter permit you to form a personal reflection on your money behaviors and distinguish areas of enhancement. The entrepreneurial and investment stories that are shared throughout the book offer assistance to you in understanding the procedures utilized by successful people to engage you to create way better financial choices.

This book is specifically for teenagers like you who are dreaming of a life filled with adventure and excitement but are held back by the chains of financial uncertainty. For teenagers like you who are tired of feeling that their financial destiny is not in their hands and are ready to head life in the direction of their dreams, this book provides all the information needed to tackle these issues smoothly.

Through this book, I want you all to gain financial prosperity as a teenager. I am confident that if you implement these strategies, you will be guaranteed a life with fewer financial worries.

As you start reading, you will be introduced to borrowing money, taxes, and another financial services. Each of these will be dealt with in detail.

As I have been chapping about personal finance and financial stability, let me assure you that in this book, you will not only be reading about the strategies. I want to make sure you get a better idea about the basics of personal finance.

I will discuss the basics of all concepts related to personal finance. This guide will also explore the significance of building a saving culture and understanding the best saving practices.

In this book, I have also covered debt management, providing insights into the difference between good and bad debt and getting out of it. You will further be familiarized with the concept and importance of credit reports so that you learn how to build, maintain, and repair a healthy credit profile.

This guide will help you step into the world of investments and understand concepts in it. Moreover, it also explores investment risks and returns.

Lastly, this guide will teach you ways to increase your income, shed light on part-time jobs, develop and monetize skills, and invest in your career and entrepreneurship ideas.

Remember to be extra vigilant in this hustle of achieving financial freedom and do not let the shine of money betray you as Plato said:

"The greatest wealth is to live content with little."

To gain true wealth, you must understand that having money and possessions doesn't count. Instead, true wealth comes from the understanding of gratitude and simplicity. Although financial success is important, it's equally essential to stay joyful in the simplest life's pleasure.

So, do you want to join me on the journey to financial freedom? Do you want me to guide you to a financially secure future? If yes, then get on reading this first-hand guide with me and understand the concept of personal finance in depth.

Ask Yourself

1. What does SMART represent as a reference to setting goals?
a) Simple, Meaningful, Achievable, Realistic and Timely.
b) Specific, Measurable, Achievable, Relevant and Time-bound.
c) Strategic, Motivating, Aligned, Realistic, Time-bound.
d) Specific, Measurable, Achievable, Relevant, and Time-bound.

2. Which of these is an example of a SMART financial goal?
a) "I would like to be rich."
a) "I will save $100/month to go on a vacation next summer."
c) "In the future, I will have a luxury car."
d) "One day, I would love to travel the world."

3. Why do we need to consider our financial goals in the context of short-term, mid-term, and long-term objectives?
a) It lends credibility to the fact that there is more flexibility in goal realization.
b) It assists in the prioritization of objectives by considering the timeliness and the significance of those tasks.
b) It guarantees goal processability and feasibility.
d) All of the above.

4. What is one possible benefit of SMART financial goal-setting?
a) It helps to arrive at the goals.
b) It implies a possibility of being more straightforward with objectives.
c) It makes for immediate victory.
d) It doesn't require one to track progress.

5. Which of the following is NOT a feature of a SMART financial objective?
a) Specific
b) Measurable
c) Ambiguous
d) Time-bound

CHAPTER 1

Personal Finance Basics

"There is no true freedom without financial freedom."
— Ralph Waldo Emerson

I. Understanding Personal Finance

IMAGINE YOU ARE on the coastline of a vast ocean, with waves crashing ashore and the horizon far away in the distance. Now think of each wave as a financial decision you will have to make during your lifetime: some of them trivial, others huge. How will you find your way through these waves? How will you stay calm and look for opportunities within challenges that will push you toward financial achievements?

Let me help you find the answers to these questions.

First and foremost, let's familiarize ourselves with the fundamental concepts of personal finance. This will be your roadmap through your exploration of financial literacy and independence. Just like a sailor skillfully navigating challenging waves, you will be able to manage money with ease and confidence after you have mastered these concepts.

Personal finance is a term you frequently get to hear. Understanding how it works is important for your success. Personal finance is a process of bringing your income and expenses in line with your financial situation and then creating a spending and saving budget.

Since you teenagers are on the verge of becoming adults, financial management is a valuable skill and a milestone on your way to ensuring a safe future.

Personal finance, as a discipline, includes strategies for the future in addition to the present. Gaining a strong understanding of personal finance basics before leaving college will ensure that you remain financially stable throughout your life. Be it for retirement savings or your dream house, the choices you make these days will decide how you are going to make a lot of money.

However, the question remains: What is personal finance, and why does it matter for teenagers like you? Kahn and Pearlin's (2006) research proved that financial burden is the main trigger of worries and grief in adults. They found that the impact of ongoing financial hardship on health is much more significant than that of other conditions that can negatively impact health in a similar way.

Therefore, the fear of upcoming expenses or the stress of earning bread may cause this financial worry, which can take a toll on mental health. The way forward here is to face your financial responsibilities upfront and create a visible blueprint.

In reality, there is no doubt that money management is a journey to control your life and where you are laid to rest. Whatever financial decision, even the slightest degree, will affect your future. That is why it is necessary to learn about money management in the early years of life and keep an eye on the financial issues at hand.

Personal finance is not just about balancing your checkbook or saving for a future vacation. It is the act of being in the driver's seat of your life and creating the strong foundation you need to achieve your goals.

By learning financial literacy, you become fit to make well-calculated decisions that benefit your future. Moreover, personal finance is a puzzle made up of five critical pieces: income, savings, expenses, investment, and insurance.

II. Income

Income is the fuel you need to keep your financial engine running, and you may get it from different sources — for example, personal allowance, part-time jobs, or even starting your own small business. Before embarking on your journey to gaining financial independence, you must first recognize the fundamental concept of managing your funds.

For instance, if you earn $50 weekly from your part-time job, rather than buying anything your heart desires on the spot, set aside a part for savings and investment in your long-term future. This minor habit can give you big gains in the long run.

III. Spending

Spending is where the practical side of personal finance comes into play. That is where you decide how to spend the money you have earned. Your expenditures matter, regardless of whether they are essential for survival, such as groceries or luxuries like buying tickets to a show or video games. Every penny you spend influences your finances. The knowledge of spending between needs and wants is essential for smart spending.

IV. Saving

Saving is disciplining yourself to keep your money for future uses or needs. It could be setting aside a sum for a new smartphone or establishing an emergency fund, which is necessary in case of unexpected expenditures or misfortunes.

Consider for a minute that you want to buy a new laptop costing $800. You can achieve your goal in 40 weeks, provided you save $20 each week from your allowance. A straightforward saving lifestyle enables you to become better off little by little without damaging your pockets.

V. Investing

Investing is like sowing seeds that develop into mighty oak trees over time. It involves spending money on things such as stocks, bonds, or real estate and making income from them. While it may seem daunting at first, investing is a means to create wealth and achieve financial growth. For instance, buying many different shares in the stock market would enable you to earn more than the inflation rate and grow your wealth over time.

VI. Protection

Finally, protection is about guaranteeing your financial safety as well as protection from sudden events or emergencies. Likewise, think of the similarity between putting on a helmet and the subsequent insurance. While the helmet protects your head from injury, insurance, and financial planning will protect your assets and future earnings from sudden risks.

Through complete and solid understanding and implementation of the five written areas of personal finance, you will be empowered to deal with all the complexities of the financial world and set yourself up for a lifetime of financial success. I am sure by now you are already thinking about making up and living large with no one limiting your possibilities.

But wait. You need to know that financial planning is also based on other principles. From understanding your earnings to planning for unforeseen events, these principles are a stepping stone to financial empowerment.

1. **Know Your Take-Home Pay:** Before committing to big expenses like credit card debt or car loans, you must first determine your net pay. You receive This money after the government takes its tax revenues, regulations, and other deductions. Identifying this number will assist you in making proper decisions about your expenditures.
2. **Prioritize Paying Yourself First:** Think about the paycheck as a pie – before dividing it into a bill and other expenses, put aside one for yourself. This means that being a saver is the best place to start. Save a part of your income to deal with the unexpected and your long-term goals like college or buying a car.
3. **Begin Your Savings Now:** Compound interest as your ally is your most reliable source of income. The sooner you start, the more time your money has to grow. Don't procrastinate – start today and contribute little by little to a savings account - remember that "small pieces can lead to great things!"
4. **Comparison of Interest Rates:** Whether it is savings or borrowings, the interest rate is scaled so that the higher it is, the more one receives, and the less one has to pay out. Rates apply to different types of savings and all credit cards, so it's worth researching them in advance.
5. **Remember the "Rule of 72":** Would you like to know how many years it will take for your money to be doubled? It is very easy to count and can be remembered by dividing 72 by the given percentage rate. In this case, your money will double within 12 years with a 6% interest rate.
6. **Don't Borrow What You Can't Pay Back:** Although borrowing loans for expensive products might be desirable, being responsible is the key. Before taking out a loan, estimate whether you will be able to make regular payments without putting any additional financial burden on yourself. Too much debt may result in a bad credit history and financial instability.

7. **Create a Budget:** Budgeting means to make the foundation of your financial success. Through income and expense tracking, you can exercise control over your finances and choose where to use your money based on findings. The budget should be interpreted as an agenda toward financial independence.
8. **Plan Your Financial Future:** Briefly outline a financial plan for yourself in which you would indicate what you want to achieve in the short and long run. It might be saving money to pay for a college education or to purchase a house, but with a plan, you will not be disrupted, and it will keep you focused on success.
9. **Buy Insurance:** Being insured for accidents and emergencies is a must since one cannot predict these events in advance. Your health, car, home, and life insurance will provide a financial cushion when an accident or unexpected event strikes.

Now that I have laid down the basics of personal finance, take a minute to envision your future…

It is one year from today. What kind of life are you looking at? What do you want to see when you reflect back? Maybe you will embark on your gap year adventure, graduate from high school with honors, or work your dream job.

Now, let's go three years out. Maybe you will fund your trip to Bali by working a summer job, or maybe the car parked in the garage is yours. Perhaps you have created a thriving small business.

Finally, let's zoom out to five years from now. What aspirations are driving you forward? Is it a career launch? Global adventure? Maybe even the keys to your own house? While those just might sound like distant dreams, whatever you pick, reaching them is actually within closer reach than you might think. Want to take those dreams into reality? If yes, grab a piece of paper or your smartphone notes app because I am providing insights on how to take your dreams into reality by setting financial goals and why it is necessary.

VII. Setting Financial Goals

Financial goals refer to the plan for managing your money wisely. When you set your financial goals, you determine your course or route for the future. It's all about deciding what you want to achieve and then putting into action a plan to get there.

But to win that treasure, you need to devise proper strategies. Similarly, proper financial planning starts with setting your goals according to the period, including short-term, mid-term, and long-term goals.

The **short-term financial** goals are actually small and achievable goals that you have set for the near future, possibly a year or even six months. They work as little stepping stones that will help you achieve those bigger goals later on. As a teenager, your short-term goals may include creating a budget, saving money for something you want, or repaying debts you owe to a friend. For example, if you aim to buy a new cell phone in six months, your short-term goal entails saving a portion of your pocket money each week until you reach your goal.

Meanwhile, **mid-term financial goals** are the ones that act as a bridge between your short-term and long-term goals. They are a bit farther to the future, typically within one to five years. These goals may include saving for a big purchase like a car or a dream vacation or investing in your education by setting aside money for college.

Lastly, **long-term financial goals** are the big-picture goals. They are the ultimate aspirations that you work toward over time. They are further down the road, usually five years or more into the future. Let's assume you dream of traveling the world after college. For this, you start investing early and regularly in the account to enjoy financial freedom and flexibility to pursue your passions later in life, which will be your long-term goal.

Some of you will say, "Why set financial goals as a teen?" This is because clear goals can give you direction and a purpose. Now, you might think setting goals will immediately lead you to success. But it isn't like this because not all goals are the same. This is where the concept of **SMART** goals comes in. **SMART** stands for Specific, Measurable, Achievable, Relevant, and Timebound.

For setting up SMART financial goals, here are five steps to help you get started:

Make Your Goal Specific: Be specific about what you want. For example, instead of saying, "I want to save money," say, "I want to save $500 to buy a new laptop."

Make Your Goal Measurable: This allows you to measure how far away you are. It could be in quantities, percentages, and other units. For example, "I intend to save $100 every month," instead of saying, "I have to save some money."

Make Your Goal Achievable: You do not have to dream less, but setting a very ambitious goal will only lead to frustration and disappointment. Try setting small goals and gradually raising them to bigger ones.

Make Your Goal Relevant: Your goal must be tightly connected with your values and priorities. Ask yourself why this goal is important and how it will improve your life.

Give Yourself a Deadline: Set a deadline. It makes it an "urgent" matter, and your focus will be up to par. For instance, "I will have saved $600 by the end of the year."

To sum up, setting SMART financial goals does not just assist you in planning, but it also leads you to a way to control your future.

VIII. Evaluating Progress Toward Financial Goals

But now, the question arises about how you will be able to identify whether your goals are worthy enough to improve your financial health. Regularly assessing your goals is vital for sustaining and guaranteeing that your finances align with them.

Monitoring and tracking are crucial parts of the process for achieving your financial goals.

Create a Budget: The budget is the first step toward accomplishing your financial goal. This will help you track income and expenses. Through this, you will understand where your money is and where you can make adjustments to save even more.

Set Up a Savings Plan: A savings plan will help you set up a certain amount of money every month to help you reach your future goals. What matters is not if you are saving for a smartphone, a car, or college, but once you have a saving plan set up, you know you are saving money for the things important to you.

Set up a Tracking System: Track your income, expenditures, savings, and investments using a spreadsheet, budgeting app, or personal financial management tool. This will show you where your finances stand, and you can achieve your progress faster by tracking your improvement.

Utilize Budgeting Tools for Monitoring Your Expenses: Budgeting tools will help you spend money wisely and remain aware of your spending as you progress toward your financial goals.

Review Consistently: The following step toward monitoring your financial goal objective is to review it routinely. Practice it regularly to review your financial plan, savings plan, and investments once every six months.

Following these steps and staying consistent in tracking your progress will make you brilliant at managing your finances appropriately and accomplishing your financial goals.

IX. Tools for Tracking Financial Goals

Financial tools are your personal finance assistants. They assist you in scheduling, accounting, directing, and tracking your investments. Whether you're saving for a huge expense, tracking your expenses, or even planning for your future, these tools will help keep your finances aligned.

Indeed, financial tools come in various forms and have different functions. From budgeting apps to investment calculators, such tools can be used for anything, from reviewing your expenses to financial planning for retirement.

But where do you start? Well, think of it like this: just as you need tools to build a house or fix a car, you need financial tools to build and maintain your financial health.

Therefore, how do you know when is the best time to begin using financial tools? Here are a few signs to look out for:
1. If you observe that you spend a lot of your time on financial duties but produce very little results, it could be the right time to automate some of the tasks.
2. If your finances become increasingly difficult to manage as your assets grow, it is most likely time to upgrade to a more advanced system.
3. If you don't understand where you are spending your money, it's time you start using the tools to help you see your money more clearly.

So, how do you select the right financial tools for yourself? Here are a few things to consider:
1. Ensure that the tools you select are convenient and simple. The idea is not to spend too much time on them to learn how to use them but actually to use them.
2. Consider tools with good security functions, as they protect your financial data from hackers.
3. It's time to consider the most important features to you—maybe budgeting, investment tracking, or something else—and then make sure the tools you use have these features.

Choosing the right financial tools is all about finding what works best for you and your unique financial situation. With the right tools in hand, you will be well on your way to mastering your money and achieving your financial goals.

But where can you find some practical financial tools, apps, and websites that can help you on your journey to personal financial management?

Here are a few:

X. Mobile Applications

In our digital age, there is an app for everything, including one for managing your finances. Here are some popular personal finance apps that are user-friendly and free:

Mint: This app tracks your spending, allows you to create budgets, and gives you specific financial insights.

You Need a Budget (YNAB): This tool helps you divide your income between particular aims and offers on-hand finance management.

Every Dollar: It provides a budgeting tool that is easy to use and enables you to control your spending.

Personal Capital: You can use it to view your investments, retirement accounts, and your net worth.

Pocket Guard: Analyze your spending history to help you find ways to be charitable.

Spendee: It tracks your inflows and outflows, categorizes your transactions, and prepares the financial reports graphically.

XI. Spreadsheets

If you're more comfortable with an interactive approach to budgeting, try Google Sheets or Microsoft Excel spreadsheets. These tools will help you design your budgeting plan and make your expense tracking as accurate as possible.

XII. Online Websites

Besides these applications and spreadsheets, there are numerous free websites on the internet you could use to improve your financial literacy and make conscious choices. Here are a few websites worth exploring:

Debt.org: It provides a complete collection of tools for debt management, credit counseling, and financial literacy.

Federal Student Aid: It offers college students and their family's information and aid resources.

You Need a Budget Blog: Its features include articles, tips, and success stories, all designed to help you control your budget and achieve your financial targets.

NerdWallet: It provides personalized financial advice, comparative tools, and expert views about credit cards, loans, and insurance.

Investopedia Dictionary: It is a crucial source for learning financial phrases and themes.

With these tools and resources, you will have the power to manage your finances in the right direction and have a secure financial future.

Now that I have laid the foundation for understanding the significance of setting SMART financial goals and monitoring your progress toward accomplishing them, it is the ideal time to move on to the next important part of personal finance: budgeting.

Just like a boat needs a compass to explore the oceans, a strong budget plan fills in as your financial compass, directing you toward your objectives and assisting you with keeping on track when confronted with difficult situations.

KEY TAKEAWAYS

- Personal finance is a process of bringing your income and expenses in line with your financial situation.
- The core areas of managing personal finance include income, spending, savings, investments, and protection.
- The principles of personal finance include knowing your take-home pay, paying yourself first, starting saving now, comparing interest rates, remembering the 'Rule of 72', never borrowing what you can't repay, creating a budget, keeping an eye on high risks, not expecting something for nothing, planning your financial future, maintaining a high credit profile, and buying insurance.
- Proper financial planning starts with setting your goals according to the timespan, including short-term, mid-term, and long-term goals.
- Smart personal finance involves developing strategies that include budgeting, creating an emergency fund, paying off debt, using credit cards wisely, saving for retirement, and much more.
- Monitoring and tracking are crucial parts of the process for achieving your financial goals. Track your financial progress by creating a budget, setting up a savings plan, setting up a tracking

system, using budgeting tools, reviewing your goals regularly, celebrating milestones, and staying patient.
- Implementing financial management tools and software provides an automated and simplified approach to managing your finances.

Exercise 1.1

FUN TO DO:

Create a list of your Short-Term, Mid-Term, and Long-Term Financial Goals, setting deadlines for each goal. Also, write the action steps you will be taking to achieve your goals.

SHORT-TERM GOALS:

_____
_____
_____

MID-TERM GOALS:

_____
_____
_____

LONG-TERM GOALS:

_____
_____
_____

ACTION STEPS:

_____
_____
_____

CHAPTER 2

All About Budgets

"Budgeting is telling your money where to go instead of wondering where it went."

I. Why Budget?

SO, THE FIRST chapter of your journey into personal finance was the introduction of a fundamental approach to money, which is about seeing the flow of money in and out of your life and the reason for setting financial goals. Now, let's engage in the practical aspect of managing your finances: budgeting – knowing where your money "goes."

Before you get into the core of budgeting, take a moment for self-reflection and ask yourself the following questions:
  a. Is your income less than your expenses
  b. Are you worried or stressed about your financial situation?
  c. Do you spend all the money you make?
  d. Do you find yourself purchasing things you do not need when you have money?
  e. Does your current income not allow you to live the life you want?

Don't worry. These questions aim not to evaluate or criticize but to enlighten you on your spending behavior and mindset.

If your answer to these questions is 'yes,' then you need to understand the essence of budgeting and its significance for ongoing financial stability.

Now, suppose your wallet is a map, and each dollar bill inside is the road that leads to various destinations. Without a plan, those dollars could take you on a rollercoaster ride, landing you in places you didn't want to end up. But no need to panic. Budgeting is like a GPS for your money – it makes your financial direction clear and helps you successfully reach destinations the way you want.

A budget is not only a piece of paper on which you write your expenses and income; it is much more than that! It is a tool for empowerment, a way to get rid of financial dependency and take control of your financial destiny.

Although budgeting is an effective way to achieve stability, several myths surround it. These myths might be what is keeping you away from making budgets. Let's debunk some of these:

1. **I Don't Have to Stick to a Budget:** Quite a lot of people believe budgeting is a special practice that only those with limited income must do. However, a budget is your instrument of financial protection as it gives you the freedom to plan and budget for your expenses and a chance to save and invest your earnings.
2. **I Struggle with Math Skills:** Thanks to the technology and user-friendly software available, the calculation of budgets is no longer a thing of the past. Just to dispel this myth, budgeting is not so much about carrying out math skills as it is about discipline and organization, and therefore, every person can do it regardless of his or her skills.
3. **I Have a Secure Job:** It is good if you are hoping for the best, but it is important to think about all the possible outcomes. In addition, you should understand that there will still be future unexpected twists, and you should be ready to deal with them. Nothing is expected to be without troubles or obstacles, and budgeting is essential as the safety net for any unpleasant phenomenon in your life.
4. **Unemployment Insurance Will Help Me Out:** I believe unemployment insurance can be helpful for you at the initial stage, but that doesn't change the fact that being careful with

your finances is still the best solution. A sensible budget will allow you to have adequate finances for the unexpected.

5. **I Don't Want to Deprive Myself:** Budgeting does not aim at deprivation; instead, it focuses on prioritization. All you need to do is make sure you spend money on what matters most in your life, and those things make you joyful without guilt if you spend money.

Now that I have mentioned some common myths associated with budgeting, let me dispel some more myths as to the reasons why making a budget is crucial for you:

1. **Helps in Achieving Long-Term Goals:** By crafting a budget, you can easily get to your long-term goals. Whether saving for college, traveling the world, or buying your favorite car, budgeting has taught you well.
2. **Saves You from Overspending:** With temptations of impulse buying and click-to-purchases all around us, overspending is a trap that often unexpectedly catches the unaware. But fear not! A well-devised budget will help you resist the temptation of pointless spending and keep you on the right course toward financial prosperity.
3. **Helps with Your Retirement Savings:** Including retirement savings in your budget from a young age is not a trial for only your golden years; it is the starting point of a safe and prosperous future.
4. **Helps to Prepare for Emergencies:** No matter how prepared you think you are; life always has its own twist off the bat at the hardest time for you. Being financially ill-equipped for a sudden urgent breakdown of a car, medical situation, or other issues of that nature can affect you a great deal financially unless you have prior preparation. In that case, it's your trustworthy emergency fund, developed with disciplined budgeting, that comes to the rescue.

II. Tracking Your Income and Spending

I hope you are clear about your need for budgeting, and I am sure you can't wait to devise a budget to continue your journey toward financial success. But remember that Rome was not built in a day, and neither can financial stability. However, the road to your financial freedom may be long, and a dose of patience, perseverance, and a little extra effort to stick to your budget plan and be comfortable with your action plan will unlock success. First off, before indulging in the details of budgeting, lay the foundation by tracking all your expenses.

Here are some benefits that will convince you to keep a close eye on your spending:

Conscious Spending: Tracking your expenses makes every dollar you spend a conscious decision—no more impulse buying. Instead, you become the boss of your own financial situation.

Financial Support: Keep track of your spending and have a gist of what your finances look like. It allows you to live without worry, and clearly, you will see where your funds come from and move to; thus, you can manage your budget well, pay off your debts, save for emergencies, and plan for future expenses.

Create the Perfect Budget: Walk along your path and make the right budget plan with your newfound power to examine your expenditures. This financial ability helps you align your income and expenses.

Cultivating the Habit of Savings: Tracking your expenses helps eliminate wasteful expenses. This encourages saving, laying the foundation for a prosperous future.

Helps in Achieving Financial Goals: Tracking your spending will help you achieve your financial goals. This mainly plays the role of eliminating unneeded expenses and, of course, saving for the things that you value most.

Here are five simple and exciting ways to track your income like a pro:
1. **Check Your Bank and Credit Card Statements:** If you're like most people who love shopping online, your bank and credit card statements serve as maps showing your shopping adventures.

Look at your spending at the end of each month. Then, find out how much you spend in different categories. It is as if you are cracking a mystery and finding patterns in your expense habits.
2. **Hold on to Those Receipts:** If you are the type of person who is more of a cash spender, don't throw away receipts. Store them in your wallet or on your phone. Calculate them at the end of the period you want to see how much you have spent. It is as simple as that! It's like collecting tokens on your financial journey and then cashing them to reveal insights into your spending habits.
3. **Get Tech-Savvy with Apps:** Is budgeting really a one-size-fits-all, or can it be techy and trendy, too? Many cool budgeting apps available today can help you reduce manual effort and make keeping track of your expenses more straightforward.
4. **Keep It Old School with Pen and Paper:** The classics are here to stay and never go out of style. Take your pen and paper and write down all your expenses as if you were a money-saving intelligence officer.
5. **Excel in Spreadsheet Mastery:** Create a spreadsheet on your computer using Excel or Google Sheets. It's so exciting when you realize that your account acts as the financial command center, showing you the amount spent and a graphical illustration of your expenditures all in one place!

Tips for Effective Tracking of Expenses:
- Set Realistic Financial Goals
- Keep Track of all Expenses, No Matter How Small
- Categorize Expenses for Better Analysis
- Review Spending Regularly and Adjust Accordingly

Some common Expense Categories in a Budget include:
- Property Taxes
- Car Payment
- Food
- Utilities
- Student Loan Payment
- Tuition Fees
- Gym Membership
- Entertainment and Hobbies
- Clothing and Personal Care
- Travel

III. Developing a Personal Budget

Now, fasten your seatbelts! Your wait is over. You have come across the importance, benefits, and ways of tracking. Here, we will understand the ways of developing a personal budget.

1. **Calculate Your Income:** You should begin by totaling all your sources of income, including your salary, any side gigs, and any investments you make. Consider it as collecting treasures from different chests that enable you to fulfill your dreams. Imagine you make $500 per week from your part-time job and $200 per month as a tutor. That is a $700 monthly income that you can now work with.

2. **List Your Expenses:** List all your expenses, starting with non-negotiables like rent and utility bills and continuing with your discretionary expenses, such as dining out and entertainment. After this, you will be able to identify the amount of money you usually make and spend every month, you can consider dividing

your expenses into various categories. Your expenses will typically fall into three categories:

Fixed Expenses: These are fixed expenses that do not change each month and are not optional, such as rent and car payments.

Variable Expenses: These are crucial fixed expenses that routinely fluctuate in price. Behavioral changes can modify these expenditures, such as buying weekly groceries and fuel for your car.

Discretionary Expenses: These expenses cover everything extra and are different for every month. They are your expenses when you go to a theatre, buy a gift for someone, or order takeout.

IV. Average Consumer Expenditure:

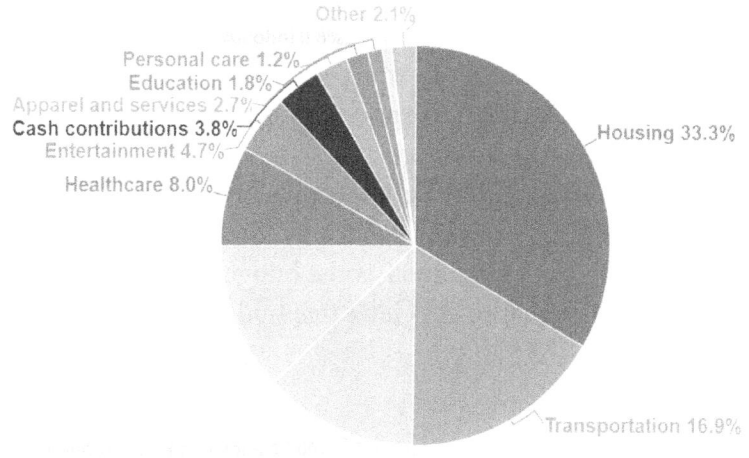

Source: Bureau of Labor fitatistics data released in 2023

1. **Set Realistic Goals:** Dream big and be ambitious. Review your short-term and long-term financial goals. Regardless of your financial objectives, like funding a dream vacation or paying off your debts, having definite targets brings you inner balance, and

you become more motivated in your budget management. Let's say your goal is to put together a $1000 fund for your summer road trip. Divide this amount into monthly savings goals to make it more attainable.

2. **Choose Your Budgeting Strategy:** Some budgeting strategy options available are the envelope system, zero-based budget, and the 50/30/20 rule. You should compare them and choose the one you are comfortable with. Consider it as a process of picking a map or an app to set your way for the travel ahead.

Envelope System: This type of strategy is ideal for first-timers since it allows budgeting for one month at a time. People who are paid in cash will also be able to use this system to keep track of their money. This system is quite easy to use; you just write on the envelopes what you intend to buy, then put the money you would expect to spend on in each of these envelopes.

Budgeting Resources:

- Budget Apps: Budgeting Apps such as Mint and Every Dollar can help with budgeting.
- Savings Accounts: Find an account that earns a competitive annual percentage yield.
- Budget Calculator: Get a good home budget calculator.
- Microsoft Office Template: Get a free budget template with Microsoft 365.

Zero-based budget: This is sometimes referred to as the zero-sum budget. In essence, it is a method of budget management that justifies every penny spent. As all your money disappears in your expenditures, savings, and debt repayment, none of it gets piped out. When you do your budgeting, whatever amount of money is left after all the expenditures, you have to either tag it to the next month's budget or set it aside in another category.

50/30/20 budget: By using this strategy, you can divide our income into two major groups: needs and wants. So, about 50% goes to what you need, 30% goes to nice things you want, and the remaining 20% goes to savings and debt repayment. This budgeting system allows you to pay toward debt and gives some leeway for occasions in which you can indulge and cash flow to manage unforeseen expenses.

3. **Adjust Your Habits:** Let's examine how you spend your money and how to change your spending patterns to fit into your budgeting plan. It is as if you are adjusting your compass to keep you on the path to financial prosperity. For example, if you can reduce the number of take outs and cook at home more often, your savings will increase!
4. **Track Your Progress:** Follow your budget and set a schedule for achieving your goals. Celebrate your achievements, and never be afraid to modify the plan when necessary.

V. Reducing Unnecessary Expenditures

While devising a budget, you will encounter unnecessary expenditures. It's important to cut out unnecessary spending to keep your budget on track and make the most of your money.

Consider these strategies to eliminate unnecessary spending from your money:

1. **Understanding Your Financial Situation:** Just as you plot your coordinates on a map, tracking your expenses offers insight into your financial situation. By grasping where your money flows, you can steer clear of unnecessary expenditures and remain aligned with your budgeting journey.
2. **Prioritizing Essential Expenses:** While it is important to stick to the budget, don't overlook the little things that are either a priority or that give you pleasure. Strive to align your spending with your principles, and you will be able to strike the perfect balance between budgeting and personal gain.

3. **Maximizing "Monthly" Opportunities:** Streamline monthly expenditures by reassessing subscriptions and recurring costs. Whether pausing gym memberships or trimming takeout expenses, discover ways to reduce monthly expenses without compromising financial goals.
4. **Minimizing Interest Expenses:** Look at interest rates and ways to prevent loan costs from going up. Shifting to an additional personal payment not only yields long-term but equally fastens your way toward financial freedom.

VI. Sticking to your Budget

In your financial journey up to now, I have told you the ways of devising a budget and eliminating unnecessary expenditures. But just think for a minute: what if you put in a lot of time and effort to create a budget, following all the tips and tricks I have given you, but you still can't quite stick to the budget? What will you do then? You will open your very own guide to personal finance and look for the ways I am telling you to stick to the budget. So, let's start with how to stick to your budget.

Limit Credit Card Usage: Choose a lower credit limit to control impulse spending, which results in high-interest debts. Students should understand their spending habits and learn to budget their expenses within the credit limit. Don't waste a penny on unnecessary things. Invest everything for a bigger purpose, such as savings or debt clearance.

Budget to Zero: For all income earned, assign every penny for spending or savings. Therefore, you learn to have full control and flexibility in your budgeting attitude.

Embrace No-Spend Challenges: Set yourself a self-denial challenge by not spending on non-essential items for a certain timeframe. Look for an accountability partner to keep it fun and exciting.

Clarify Savings Goals: Set your saving goals, whether a car, a deposit for a house, or a dream vacation. Passion-oriented and clearly defined goals increase the ability to stick to the budget.

Prioritize Self-Payment: Deduct money from your salary first and put it in your savings or toward debt eradication; this will help you not overspend.

Buddy Up for Budgeting: Connect to someone who can hold you to your goals, like a friend or a family member, to help you stay on track with your financial plan or budget. Cooperation makes budgeting a hobby that not only attracts but also gives an impression of excellence.

I am sure these strategies will make you stick to your budget at any cost.

So, finally, you have passed the route to budgeting with me. But don't put your financial compass down. In the next chapter, I will make you dig into the great world of setting a saving culture, exploring the codes to saving, grasping the most appropriate ways for saving effectively, and devising your saving plan that suits your goals and objectives. On top of that, I will help you learn how to utilize compounding to your benefit and understand how inflation plays a role. So, what are you looking for? Come, power up your savings with me!

KEY TAKEAWAYS

- Budgeting is the foundation of financial success, providing a roadmap for managing income and expenses and saving effectively.
- Several myths surround a budget, including struggling with math, thinking your job is secure, thinking employment insurance will help you out, not wanting anything significant, and more.
- Dispelling myths around budgeting and recognizing it as a powerful tool for achieving financial goals, reducing stress, and gaining control over your finances.
- Implementing strategies to track your income and spending accurately, enabling you to make informed financial decisions and identify areas for improvement.
- Explore various personal budget development methods, from traditional pen-and-paper approaches to modern digital tools and apps.

- Learn practical tips for cutting back on unnecessary expenses, which will allow you to allocate more funds toward savings and financial goals.
- Embrace strategies for sticking to your budget, including setting realistic goals, automating savings, and cultivating a mindset of mindful spending.

Exercise 2.1

FUN TO DO!

Grab a friend or a family member and take turns role-playing different budgeting scenarios. Practice negotiating expenses, making trade-offs, and finding creative solutions to financial challenges.

CHAPTER 3

Master the Piggy Bank

"It's not how much money you make, but how much money you keep, how hard it works for you, and how many generations you keep it for."

-Robert Kiyosaki

I. Understanding Savings and Its Best Practices

SO NOW THAT you have decided to budget, saving is the next step. You might be wondering how to do this, but my guide has got you covered once again. Before we begin, it's important to ask yourself some self-reflection questions. As always, I am starting this chapter by asking about your personal finances. This is because I want you to reflect on your financial situation and find the answers you've been searching for. This will help you focus on your financial goals and take appropriate action.

Moving from budgeting to saving is a necessary step in mastering personal finance. Budgeting is the first step, as it helps you arrange your earnings and expenditures, but saving takes it a level higher by reserving some amount at all times for future purposes and goals.

So before diving into the golden rules and practices for saving, ask yourself:

1. Do you have emergency savings?

2. Do you have a savings plan for your long-term goals?

If not, you are in the right spot. Remember, all financial goals, from building an emergency fund to buying a home to preparing for retirement, share one thing in common: saving money to accomplish them.

But wait, what exactly is saving? Setting aside a part of your income for future use instead of spending all that you earn is a practice. It is like having a safety net that you can rely on in case of emergency bills or unexpected financial challenges.

Saving money gives you choices. You can dream big and run after your ambitious goals without financial pressure. Below are three reasons why you should start saving:

Financial Security: Saving money boosts your security in the future since it sets aside some cash for needy days and future expenditures. Life is full of uncertainties, but having savings as a backup allows you to pass through any storm that may come your way with confidence and tranquility.

Freedom to Take Risks: When you have money in the bank, you have the freedom to be selective and go for ventures that promise a better payoff in the future. Whenever you start owning a business, making a career change, or investing some money into new ventures, having the financial cushion helps boost your confidence in your interests without the stress of making money somewhere on the spot.

Harnessing the Power of Compound Interest: Saving money maintains wealth and bends it to the power of compound interest. As you begin to save, you will see that your savings multiply. Initially, this is due to the interest added to your initial investment, but as time progresses, this interest is also earned over the previous periods. This compounding effect is advantageous and can help the investment grow faster than inflation, making savings provide real value for money.

But the most important question is how much money you should save. Of course, it's hard to pinpoint the exact sum as it depends on many factors, ranging from your expenses to your financial circumstances. A good rule of thumb is to have at least three to six months' worth of living expenses saved in a liquid account. This gives you a safety belt in the sense that you will have a financial cushion to lean on in case of emergencies like medical bills or unemployment.

II. Creating A Savings Plan

. Creating A Savings Plan

Now that you have learned some clever ways to save and boost your financial game, let's delve into the next exciting part: creating your own savings plan.

As Benjamin Franklin said, "If you fail to plan, you are planning to fail!" Indeed, planning is a crucial step for success. So, a savings plan is like a roadmap for your money, guiding you toward specific financial goals. It outlines what you want to achieve and the steps you must take to get there. Salikin et al. (2012) state that teenagers should learn to live within their means. Expensive electronics, going out with friends, and eating out multiple times a week will likely become a thing of the past. They should meet all financial obligations before spending on frivolous items that are unnecessary for survival.

Which of your goals needs a saving plan?
- Emergency Savings
- Vacation Plans
- College Planning
- Purchasing A Vehicle
- Buying Your Favorite Gadget

https://www.investopedia.com/make-savings-plan-5208028

By saving up during your teen years, you will find it easier to cope with the changes that occur as you age. When you have a specific plan, it will facilitate the process of your financial management and achieving your targets.

Below are the steps that will definitely assist you in creating a perfect saving plan:

Step #1: Gather Your Documents: Before embarking on a savings plan, gather some primary documents, such as bank statements, utility bills, and loan statements from the preceding three months. This will ensure all information is clear and help the entire process run smoothly.

Step #2: Multiply Your Profits: Find your monthly income by adding the total from different sources, such as paychecks, freelance projects, and investment earnings. Do not ignore incorporating taxes if you have additional income like child support or investment.

Step #3: Make Financial Goals: Recognize your financial goals and what is really important to you. Define the goals that will work best for you to achieve by following your priorities. Decide whether eliminating debts, saving for a down payment, or investing for retirement is a priority.

Step #5: Make a Plan: Craft a strategy for attaining objectives by reviewing expenditures, observing savings options, or finding ways to boost income. Consider saving for non-essential spending or generating other forms of income.

Step #6: Stick to Your Plan: Achieve the dream of saving by automating payments, regularly reviewing your plan, and making amendments as needed.

By following these steps, you will be on the path to realizing your financial goals and securing a brighter future.

III. The Law of Compounding: How Your Money Grows

Along with the strategies you have adopted for your savings plan, remember how the compounding mechanism is working hard on your path to financial success. Albert Einstein said, "Compound Interest is the Eighth Wonder of the World."

The money you save today has an opportunity to turn into gold (as evidenced by the wonders of compounding). Such as sowing seeds in a garden, the earlier you start, the more time your funds have for growth. Let's go into detail about how compounding can rock your savings plan and help you build up a financial wall against risks.

Compound interest isn't just about adding the interest to your initial investment or loan amount but is also the idea of letting the interest accumulate over time. It is about drawing or giving interest on the interest you have already earned or paid.

For example, suppose you deposit $100 into an account with compound interest. After a certain period of time, $100 accumulates interest, and that interest earns a little interest as well. You could say it is like a snowball effect: You kick off with your savings, and one day, you will wake up wondering where it all came from. But here's the catch: compounding works on both sides. Although it helps you save more, interest compounds can also make it harder to pay back debt because you are paying interest on the original amount and any interest that has accumulated.

Before delving into how compounding works, let's discover its awesome perks over time and how it can supercharge your financial journey.

- **Turbocharged Growth: Picture this:** When you reinvest your earnings, your initial investment and the profits you've racked up come together to generate even more gains. This turbocharges your investment, skyrocketing your wealth over time. It's like leveling up your money game!
- **Beat Inflation:** Compounding at higher rates acts as a shield against the sneaky effects of inflation. This means your money maintains its purchasing power, keeping your financial future safe and sound.
- **Crush Your Goals:** With compounding on your side, reaching your financial goals becomes a breeze. You can easily hit your target amounts or even stash away more than you need, creating a cozy financial cushion for whatever life throws your way.

By tapping into the magic of compounding, you can maximize your investment strategies and confidently set sail toward your financial dreams.

Let me thoroughly explain it to you. Have you ever seen a tiny snowball grow into a giant snowball as it rolls down a hill? That's like your money with compounding!

Here's the lowdown on how it works:

For instance, suppose you invest Rs 10,000 at an 8% annual rate. In the first year, the sum of money multiplies by 1.8%, and you get $10,800 in hand. But in actuality, you do not take out the equivalent of $800 by investing that instead. Now, in the second year, $864 is added to the already existing investment of $10,800, which will be 8% of the second-year investment amount. This cycle keeps repeating, and your money snowballs thanks to the growing base amount. Over time, compounding works its magic, boosting your returns big time. This formula for compounding will make it more clear for you.

IV. Formula of Compounding

The formula for the Future Value (FV) of a present asset needs compound interest money as its main concept. The formula consists of two parts here: (1) Present Value and (2) inequality between the interest and compounding rates. Rate, the frequency of compounding (or the number of compounding periods) per year, and the total number of years. The generalized formula for compound interest is:

FV = PV × (1+ni)nt

Where:

FV= Future Value

PV= Present Value

i = Annual Interest Rate

n = Number of compounding periods per time period

t = The Time Period

This formula assumes that no additional changes outside of interest are made to the original principal balance.

I hope the law of compounding is crystal clear to you. I know you must be desperate to harness its full power. If so, check out these awesome strategies!

- **Early Bird Wins:** Start investing early! Compounding loves time, so the earlier you begin, the more time your investments have to grow. Plus, toss in regular contributions (like monthly or quarterly), and you'll turbocharge the compounding effect by consistently boosting your initial investment.
- **Reinvest Like a Boss:** When your investments score dividends or capital gains (fancy terms for extra cash), don't cash out — reinvest! This turbocharges your compounding power, leading to even juicier returns over time. It's like planting seeds and then planting more seeds from the fruits they bear!
- **Go for Growth:** Choose investments with serious growth potential. Think stocks or mutual funds known for their stellar performance over time. You'll boost your compounding power by carefully selecting your investment and observing the amazing wealth increase. Just make sure to do your homework and select the strategies that meet your objectives and risk level. On a venture of compounding, you should try to be patient. So be thoughtful, remain disciplined, and see how your money gradually keeps multiplying over time!

V. The Effect of Inflation on Your Savings

All right, let's break down inflation: It means that over time, the costs of such goods as food, clothes, and gadgets rise higher than the money increases. Imagine this situation as your pocket money decreases, as inflation does not let you buy the same amount of stuff as earlier.

Now, let's see what changes happen when inflation rises.

But here's the scoop: invest wisely, and what you save will become more valuable than inflation can take. So, while all pocket money deflates out of their money, yours remains survivable, allowing you to still have a cool lifestyle.

Now, let me explain the reasons for the price inflation. Here are the main reasons behind inflation:
1. **High demand, low supply:** It is quite a simple idea, but it gets everyone challenging themselves to obtain the latest smartphone even when there aren't enough for a rapid price hike to Instagram likes when you win a giveaway.
2. **Pricey imports:** Supposedly, the cost of importing raw materials for your favorite sneakers will double, making them more expensive than collector's edition items.
3. **Rising production costs:** In the end, customers pay more because firms have to keep raising prices to remain profitable.
4. **Fat paychecks:** When consumers make more money and have extra cash, companies become much more confident about increasing product prices. It's like everyone is in a generous mood to give more gifts.
5. **Productivity slump:** If businesses aren't producing goods in enough quantities, they can raise their prices to compensate for the drop in profit.

By now, I am sure you have an outline of the calamities inflation can bring. But still, let this guide inform you of how inflation affects your savings.
1. **Eroding Savings:** Inflation is a silent thief, stealthily reducing the worth of your savings and deposits, and you might not realize this until it is too late. The fact that your money only stays safe if it is in the bank won't save you from the consequences of inflation as prices keep growing. On the one hand, imagine you have saved $10,000 to cover for one or two months when something goes wrong. As the inflation stands at 2.5% annually, the $10,000 in the future will buy you much less. And in a decade, you are looking at $7,812 in your pocket. Skip to 25 years later, and the $10,000 you have been saving might be worth only $5,394.
2. **Reduced Spending Power:** Inflation will be the most powerful enemy of your power of spending. Higher costs of groceries and utilities make it impossible for your money to last as long as

it used to. For example, the most apparent changes caused by inflation are the higher food and fuel bills.
3. **Impact on Savings:** While savings in cash accounts give no guarantee of value preservation, inflation tends to outstrip interest rates, rendering the savings worthless. In such a scenario, it will be harder for your savings to hold a steady increase, leading to less access to goods and services you need to buy.

Feeling unmotivated? If yes, let this guide led you to some ways to fight inflation. Here are a few ways to reduce the impact of inflation on your savings.
1. **Savvy Spending Choices:** You can battle inflation with insightful spending choices. Rather than going overboard on things inclined to cost climbs, they can select items less impacted by expansion. For instance, picking plant-based proteins over animal-based proteins at the supermarket can offer investment funds amid rising food costs.
2. **Safeguarding Savings:** To protect your savings from the erosive impacts of expansion, you can look for better yields on their speculations. By investigating investment options, you might procure more significant yields than overwhelm inflation, defending the worth of your cash. To sum up, inflation is a financial force that influences everybody, including teenagers like yourself. As the cost of goods and services rises over the long term, it's fundamental for you to be proactive in dealing with your savings to alleviate the effect of inflation.

KEY TAKEAWAYS

- Saving money is a crucial instrument in developing assets and guaranteeing financial stability.
- Budgeting, tracking income and spending, and lowering unnecessary expenditures constitute the core of effective savings management.
- A savings plan is a specific set of financial goals and the steps needed to reach them.
- Preparing a savings plan involves several essential requirements: documentation of important documents, income planning, tracking expenses, establishing savings goals, and a plan to achieve them.
- Compound interest is about earning or owing interest on the interest you have already earned or paid.
- Compounding further enhances savings growth potential at an exponential rate because the existing principal interests, in addition to the new principal interests, earn interest.
- Starting early, purposefully investing every month, and reinvesting dividends and capital gains are the ways to harness the force of compounding.
- A rise in inflation means an increase in the cost of goods and services.
- Inflation erodes the purchasing power of money over time, leading to a decline in the real value of savings.
- The main reasons behind inflation are high demand, low supply, pricey imports, rising production costs, fat paychecks, and productivity slump.
- To combat inflation, individuals can adjust spending habits, explore investments with higher returns, and protect their savings.

Exercise 3.1

Fun Activity: Savings Challenge

1. **Choose a Savings Goal:** Choose a small dream goal you intend to save toward. It could be a concert, a new game, or a weekend trip with your friends.
2. **Set a Deadline:** Identify the timeframe you are willing to work within to reach your target. Make it as realistic as possible but not so easy that it would demotivate you.
3. **Track Your Spending:** Record all your expenditures for a week by using a notebook or an expense app you can download on your smartphone. Discover the areas in which you can cut down to stash more cash.
4. **Create a Savings Plan:** Based on your spending analysis, put together a savings plan indicating the amount of money you need to budget for every month or week until you reach your goal.
5. **Get Creative with Saving:** Use your imagination to boost your savings by selling off unused stuff online, doing odd jobs in your neighborhood, or joining an interesting saving challenge with friends.
6. **Be Accountable:** Tell a friend or family member about your savings goal, ask them to cheer you on, and keep track of your success. Use an already-established piggy bank or track your savings visually.
7. **Celebrate Milestones:** Celebrate tiny steps along the way. For example, once you set aside 25%, then set aside 50% or 75% of your target amount. Reward yourself with a small purchase to keep your motivation high.
8. **Reflect and Adjust:** At the challenge's end, reflect on your savings. What goal did you attain? What did you learn about finance and saving money? Apply this experience to set your future savings goals while working toward responsible financial management

CHAPTER 4

Good Debt vs. Bad Debt

"Money is a good servant but a bad master."
-Bible (Matthew 25: 22-30).

CONSIDER YOURSELF A high school senior with dreams as big as the sky. From launching a tech startup to traveling the world, your ambitions know no bounds. But as graduation looms closer, so does the specter of debt.

It all starts innocently – a few credits card splurges here, a student loan application there, and before you know it, the weight of debt begins to bear down, casting a shadow over your once bright future.

One day, as you sit down to calculate the total amount owed, the numbers stare back like accusing shadows. With each digit, the reality of a debt overload becomes clearer. The dreams of entrepreneurship and adventure seem farther away than ever before.

Then you come across this personal finance guide, and you refuse to be defeated. With determination burning bright, you embark on a journey to reclaim financial freedom, armed with newfound knowledge about borrowing and debt management. From distinguishing between good and bad debt to implementing strategies to climb out of the abyss, you learn that the path to financial independence is not without its challenges, but with perseverance and the right tools, anything is possible.

Now that you have imagined yourself in this situation and have considered this guide as your savior from drowning in debt, it's my responsibility to meet your expectations.

But first things first, ask yourself these questions:
- Do you have any outstanding loans?
- Could you get a loan within the next weeks without difficulty?
- Does your financial situation cause problems with your family and friends?

These questions haunt you, don't they? Money is related to many things, including relationships, stress levels, and well-being. It is time to reflect on your answers. Are you confident with your financial position, or are there areas in need of further help?

In this chapter, I am going to guide you through borrowing and managing debt, beginning with a clear comprehension of the distinction between good and bad debts. I will help you understand the nuances of student debt, how it works, and how to safely use it without ending up in financial trouble. Lastly, the discussion on debt settlement strategies will focus on practicable approaches to getting out of debt and regaining control of your financial future. It's time to start managing your money in your own unique way!

I. Difference Between Good and Bad Debt

Hey, teens! Now, you are here to learn more about borrowing and debt. One thing to keep in mind: not all debt is equal. Yep, you heard me right! Understandably, you may think debt is always negative, but the truth is there is more to it. If debt is managed carefully, it can be useful. However, before you start using that credit card like there is no tomorrow, let's discuss the difference between good debt and bad debt and how learning about the classification can help you achieve financial prosperity.

Good debt is the superhero of finances; it comes to your aid while working toward your dreams and goals. As long as you know how to use it properly, the right debt can give you freedom and ease of mind and

open up a new door with a sea of opportunities. The following are the key features that make debt "good":
1. **Debt with a Purpose:** This, alongside the functions of education and governance, provides a variety of new mechanisms for a democratic system that handles new obstacles in modern societies that are constantly changing. Think of a time you borrowed money to finance the purchase of a home, pursue higher education, or initiate a venture. This is the type of debt you'd like to get into. This is called "good debt." These investments are not cheap, but in the long run, they grow and help you earn money, build your capital, and most importantly, reduce your tax liabilities.
2. **Building Your Future:** Good debt isn't only about spending but also about investing in yourself and your life prospects. Student loans to finance your education and a mortgage to make a house your sweet home come to mind as examples of the role debt plays in our lives. These debts are not just money deals; they are access to personal and career development.
3. **Responsible Credit Use:** Good credit management is the starting point for tapping into the potential of good debts. Being prompt with payments and paying toward your credit can help you raise your credit score, which will allow you to get lower interest rates and better financial chances.

II. Examples of Good Debt

Mortgages: Buying a house to build net worth and benefit from tax breaks.

Student Loans: Save from your daily income and invest it in educational and professional growth. This will significantly increase your chance of getting a better job with higher earnings.

Small-Business Loans: Fueling entrepreneurial ventures and spawning wealth creation.

Personal Loans: Combining loans or taking out loans for essential things prudently.

Credit Cards: Having a good credit history and being rewarded by being a responsible user.

Now, let's introduce the main culprit of the financial world — **bad debt**. Unlike good debt, bad debt can potentially destroy your finances and ruin your future life. Here are the reasons why you have to avoid this type of debt.

1. **Debt Without Benefits:** Bad debt is often associated with borrowing money to buy goods that do not have lasting benefits and depreciate in time. Indulging in products like luxurious stuff is good in the short run but can't be said to benefit your wealth in the long run.
2. **High Costs, Low Returns:** Borrowing money with a bad debt will result in the headache of paying high interest, unfavorable repayment terms, or both. Payday loans and credit card debts illustrate such traps because they make people pay more interest and live with the constant stress of unpaid debts.
3. **Risky Business:** Borrowing money without a clear idea of what to do with the funds or how you will pay for it is a risky financial game. Being in deep credit card debt can cause problems, such as increased budget strain, a decline in credit rating, and loss of financial stability. It's a high-stakes bet and one that's probably not worth it.

III. Examples of Bad Debt

Unchecked Credit Card Debt: Carrying high-interest debts without any strategy to pay them back.

Payday Loans: Small, short-term, high-interest loans that create a debt trap for borrowers during extended periods.

Upside-Down Loans: Having more loan debt than the asset's value causes financial problems.

Car Title Loans involve risking the loss of the vehicle for a small amount of cash in the hope of being able to pay back the debt.

Table 1: Good Debt vs. Bad Debt

If your debt is...	Then...
30% or less of your pre-tax income	You're in good shape
Between 31% and 36%	You're doing OK
Between 37% and 40%	Beware, you're on the borderline
More than 40%	Red flag warning

Taking On Student Debt

A student loan is like a lifeline, a financial instrument designed to help cover your college expenses. It makes college education affordable for many students around the country. But here's the catch: Unlike scholarships or grants, a student loan is borrowed money you will have to pay back eventually.

Therefore, while it may feel like winning the lottery to receive scholarships and grants, student loans come with a catch. It is a loan, not free money.

While the majority of students obtain student loans to pay for their education, careful planning and budgeting will help you become a master of the student loan system. First, let's explore the different types of student debt.

DID YOU KNOW?

The concept of student loans dates back to ancient Rome. Roman Emperor Augustus established a state-sponsored fund called the "Fiscus Judaicus" to provide interest-free loans to deserving students in the provinces of the Roman Empire.

IV. Federal Student Debt

1. *Direct Subsidized Loans* are like a piece of gold for undergraduate students with financial gaps. During your studies, you will be getting subsidized payments, and for the principal payment, you will have to start repaying the loan.
2. *Direct Unsubsidized Loans* can be used by both undergraduate and graduate students. This particular loan is not based on financial requirements. Unlike the subsidized loan, you return the interest yourself from day one, and thus, keeping up with the payments is crucial.
3. *Direct PLUS Loans* are for graduate students or parents with child dependents. This loan is simple. You just need to be ready to go through some additional steps, such as passing the credit check.
4. *Direct Consolidation Loans* can be life-saving if you manage single federal student loans. They collect all your loans in one, simplifying the repayment process. It becomes easier to trace and solve your financial obligations. However, even if your monthly payments drop, you may still pay more in the long run.

V. Private Student Debt

Now, we will get to the Wild West of student debt– private debt. These are issued by banks, schools, colleges, or universities and accompany a completely different set of rules. Unlike federal loans, private loans are often expensive and charge higher interest rates. Besides, there's a high probability that you'll start paying interest on that loan while you're still in college – oh no!

Here is a breakdown of how student loans work:

When you are thinking about attending college, student loans can be financial aid. Whether from the government or a personal lender, you will be accepting money in advance to pay for your tuition, class materials, and all those pizza deliveries you get late at night.

Things Student Loans Can Be Used For:
1. College tuition and fees
2. Book and supplies
3. Computers and other needed technology
4. Lab fees
5. Groceries
6. Study abroad expenses
7. Car expenses
8. Miscellaneous personal expenses (like bedding, a microwave, eating out, clothes, etc.)

The type of student loan you have will determine whether you pay interest and how you pay the loan. If it comes from the federal government, there might be a grace period after graduation, meaning you don't have to make the payments until you find a job. Also, the government provides help with the interest fee for a while. Yet, in the case of a private loan, you may have to deal with higher interest rates and less flexible repayment policies. Oh, and the last thing – don't forget about cosigners – they're on the hook if you can't pay up.

But the big question is: **Is student loan debt worth it?**

For many students, borrowing is the key that opens doors to career paths that promise a brighter future and financial stability.

Student loan debt can be worth it if you follow a few fundamental principles:

1. **Complete Your Education:** The first step is to complete what you have initiated. You must complete your four-year degree or a graduate program, regardless of the type of education you enroll for, to reap the expected financial benefits.
2. **Invest in Marketable Degrees:** Not all degrees have a similar structural design. Communicate with the professionals in your field and do some research to learn about your future career and expected income so that you can take smart actions and save time and money.
3. **Borrow Wisely:** Regarding the educational loans for postgraduate or specialized training, be sure about what you are starting. Think through possible earnings, repayment terms, and working capital choices before toppling heavy debt on your shoulders.

This is how to get yourself a student debt if you find yourself in need:

1. **Fill Out the FAFSA:** First, to obtain federal student loans, students must fill out the FAFSA (Free Application for Federal Student Aid). This form captures your and your parents' financial details (if you are a dependent) and sends them to your preferred schools.
2. **Receive Your Financial Aid Offer:** After processing your FAFSA, the financial aid offices of various schools' compile information, use their knowledge, and then determine the amount of aid you qualify for.
3. **Figure out Your Choices:** It's crucial to distinguish between grants/scholarships (free cash) and loans (cash you need to repay). While grants and awards resemble winning the big stake, credits accompany surprises.

Now that you have explored the steps for signing up for student debt, you must know the various options for repaying student debt because, let's face it, understanding **your repayment options** is just as important as borrowing the money in the first place.

VI. Repaying Federal Debts

1. **Standard Repayment Plan:** These are the payments made to the government or your mortgage lender as per the schedule given. This schedule sets out a fixed monthly amount you must pay for ten years.
2. **Graduated Repayment Plan:** Initially, the payments are lower, but soon, they will slowly rise, and the target is to erase them within ten years.
3. **Extended Repayment Plan:** For people who owe more than $30,000 in full repayment, this plan extends the stimulus payment period beyond the regular ten or 25 years.
4. **Income-Based Repayment Plan:** Each year, you would pay back a percentage of your total income, with whatever is left to forgive after 20 to 25 years of service.
5. **Income-Contingent Repayment Plan:** This resembles an income-based plan except that it takes up 20% of the remaining income and comes with the option to apply for Parent PLUS Loans.
6. **Pay As You Earn (PAYE) Repayment Plan:** The monthly payment plan requires you to pay 10% of your after-tax earnings, but the total must not be higher than the standard repayment plan.
7. **Saving on a Valuable Education (SAVE) Plan:** This plan has been recently updated, and now it provides a higher income exemption and no unpaid interest accumulation. That means that the monthly payment for the borrower can be lower.

VII. Repaying Private Debts

The lender determines the payback schedule for private student debt. Most of the time, you'll have to pay back a specific amount each month, which is a combination of principal and interest.

In the unlikely event that the terms become different, you will need to talk to the lending party again.

STATISTICS
1. Over 44 million Americans have student loan debt averaging around $32,731 per borrower.
2. Student loan debt has increased by over 102% in the past decade, making it the second-largest consumer debt category after mortgages.
3. Around 14% of student loan borrowers default on their loans within the first three years of repayment.
4. Over 65% of college seniors who graduated from public and private nonprofit colleges in 2019 had student loan debt.
5. Approximately 8.5 million student loan borrowers are in default, with many more struggling to make payments.

We will now explore **some potential pitfalls of student debt** borrowing. These must be thoroughly known since understanding them is vital in managing your finances.

1. **Impact on Grad School:** Student debt overload may turn you away from graduate-level education for financial reasons. This might reduce your career opportunities and diminish your future earnings because some professions require higher academic credentials for well-paid positions.
2. **Challenges Buying a Home:** An unrestricted student debt can lead to a salary shortage, which may deny you a chance to save the down payment for a house, and entering homeownership is impossible.
3. **Lowered Net Worth:** College loans are debt you must pay after graduating, which eventually affects your net worth by reducing it. In general, financial debts erode your position of wealth, weaken your standing to open new investment avenues, and

reduce your capacity to build other sources of income in the long run.
4. **Credit Score Damage:** When a student loan is late, or a payment is missed, it may damage your credit score; consequently, it may be difficult for you to get good interest rates on future loans, and insurance rates may also be affected.
5. **Permanent Debt:** Unlike other debts, student loans are usually not discharged through bankruptcy, which means you will be accountable for repayment even if you are in a difficult financial situation.

VIII. Avoiding Debt Overload

Now that you understand the pitfalls of student debt borrowing, it is time to actively think about the strategies to avoid debt overload. Even though tapping into borrowing for education in return for a better future may be necessary sometimes, it is also vital to carefully consider the situation. Debt overload can become a reality if you lack an effective debt management strategy and are forced to make decisions without knowledge of finances. So, shall we consider some practical ways to avoid being taken in by debts?

1. **Evaluate Your Budget:** Creating and keeping a budget is one of the most important things you can do to avoid money problems and avoid being overloaded with debt. First, review your paychecks and bills to evaluate whether your sources of income are enough to pay off the amounts you owe.
2. **Keep Debt in Check:** To avoid financial issues going forward, you should be aware of the balance between your debts and credit availability so that your safety is guaranteed. The method is to pay your existing debt as fast as possible and not play with debt.
3. **Prioritize Debt Repayment:** Focus on first paying off high-debt interest to minimize the interest payment and speed up your debt repayment journey. With paying off debts into focus, you get the obvious chance to slowly drop down the total amount you have to pay, which is a big step toward financial freedom.

4. **Restricting the Use of Credit Cards:** Having multiple credit cards is bound to increase your tendency to spend more and perhaps incur even more debt. Do not keep numerous cards with you, or you will be more prone to spend more.
5. **Strike a Deal with Your Creditors:** If you find it difficult to meet your credit obligations, don't hesitate to discuss alternative repayment plans with your creditors. Usually, creditors are open for negotiations to make lower interest rates, extended payment terms, or even the reduced amount you have to pay back. One of the simplest methods to ease the financial load is communication with creditors.

Implementing these strategies into your financial management approach is the way that can help improve your ability to avoid debt overload.

IX. Getting Out of Debt

Moving from the tactics to eliminate debt overflow to the methods that can free us from debts, you need to recognize that despite your efforts, debt can sometimes be overwhelming. Even though proactive measures can help to avoid getting into a debt trap, unforeseen events and past financial decisions may still lead to debt situations that are difficult to handle. Knowing the pitfalls of debt overload over the long term and the necessary measures for debt elimination gives you the power to move decisively in your pursuit of a financially prosperous future.

1. **Build Your Safety Net:** Life is riddled with surprises, and wise people, as a rule, put aside a small part of their income for unforeseen expenditures. Instead of using your credit cards for emergencies, save some cash for different situations – your emergency fund.
2. **Employ the Debt Snowball or Avalanche Method:** The debt snowball or avalanche method may also be a great option. Determining where and how to get out of debt may be a tough challenge that may entrap you in the cycle of stress. Go right

ahead and start with the debt snowball or the debt avalanche repayment strategies.

Debt Snowball Method: The debt snowball technique goes further because it creates a snowball effect in which you gain extra funds once you pay the minimum on all your debts and then put the extra funds toward the smallest debts. Here, you can notice a gradual decline in weight as the lowest balances are cleared first, followed by the rest.

Debt Avalanche Method: As the name implies, a debt avalanche saves you more in interest if you pay the standard payment to all the other debts and channel the remaining funds toward that with the highest interest rate. Start with the highest rate account; all funds flow after the costliest account is retired. Faithfully apply the next highest rate to the account until it is fully repaid.

3. **Embrace Frugal Living:** Living frugally will allow you to set aside money to get out of debt. Assess your spending habits and look for places to trim or eliminate spending on unnecessary things. Saving money in this way and directing that to debt repayment will speed up the way to financial freedom.
4. **Avoid Taking on New Debt:** By paying off old debt, avoid taking on new ones, as that might disrupt your process of paying off the old debt. Tear up the credit cards, remove yourself from those tempting offers, and concentrate on what you have instead of what you can't afford, which is an easy way to stay out of more debt.

In the next chapter, I will help you navigate your credit score. So, if you are excited to know what's in your credit report or how your credit score is calculated, stay tuned with your guide!

KEY TAKEAWAYS

- Good debt is an investment in your future, like a student loan or mortgage, while bad debt is expensive loans that are not important, such as credit cards.
- Bad debt can potentially affect your finances and even ruin your future life.
- When seeking student loans, evaluate the investment rate of return by forecasting potential earnings and career growth.
- Types of student debt include federal student debt and private student debt.
- Investigate all possible sources of financial aid, such as scholarships, grants, and Work-Study programs, to secure the least possible amount of debt through loans.
- Student debt can be worth it if you complete your education, invest in marketable degrees, do your homework, and borrow wisely.
- Understanding your repayment options is just as important as borrowing the money in the first place.
- Try to use a credit card for your pre-planned expenses, but stay away from cash advances and keep your cards under control.
- Keep track of your spending and consider using a master sheet or budgeting app to monitor your money situation.
- You can get out of debt by building an emergency fund, prioritizing debt repayment, employing the debt snowball or debt avalanche method, embracing frugal living, employing windfall payments, seeking financial counseling, staying committed, and avoiding taking on new debt.

Exercise 4.1

FINANCIAL FREEDOM QUIZ

1. What is the difference between good debt and bad debt?

a) good debt is money you owe for essential purchases, while bad debt is for non-essential items.

b) good debt helps you build wealth or invest in your future, while bad debt comes from unnecessary purchases with high-interest rates.

c) good debt is borrowed from family or friends, while bad debt is borrowed from financial institutions.

2. Which of the following is an example of good debt?

a) payday loans

b) credit card debt for luxury purchases

c) student loans for education

3. What should you consider when taking on student loans?

a) only consider the immediate financial burden, not the long-term benefits.

b) explore all available financial aid options, including scholarships and grants.

c) take on as much debt as possible to have extra money to spend on college.

4. How can you avoid debt overload?

a) always use credit cards for cash advances.

b) limit the number of credit cards you have to only one.

c) regularly assess your budget, avoid cash advances, and keep track of expenses.

5. What is a strategy for getting out of debt?

a) continue to accumulate more debt to maintain a lifestyle beyond your means.

b) develop a structured repayment plan and prioritize debts based on interest rates.

c) ignore your debts and hope they go away on their own.

CHAPTER 5

The Creditor's Quests

"An investment in knowledge pays the best interest."
— Benjamin Franklin

CONGRATULATIONS ON MASTERING the art of debt management! Now, it's time to level up your financial game. Yes, it's the time to explore the next frontier of financial literacy: your credit score. Have you ever questioned how creditors manage to determine whether you're a reliable borrower? Do you have any idea what a credit report is? We have the answers to these questions and more. Get ready to uncover the mysteries of your credit report and learn how to wield your score like a financial superhero. Hang tight as we explore the ins and outs of credit reports, demystify credit scores, and discover how you can turbocharge your financial future by mastering the secrets of creditworthiness!

I. What Is a Credit Report and Why Is It Important?

A credit report is a comprehensive risk profile of your financial functioning that discloses your past and present financial standing. It gives the complete picture of your lending activities, including every detail about your debt payments, unpaid balance, and the status of your existing lines of credit. Not only will your school report card indicate your academic abilities, but your credit report will also showcase how responsibly you have managed your loans and credit cards.

View it as a summary of all your recent past and present debts, which represents the main points of your credit accounts, your credit report, and other important data about credit limits.

Before we discuss the importance of credit reports, let me clarify the **difference between a credit report and a credit score.**

II. Credit Report

Think of your credit report as a comprehensive dossier that traces all the twists and turns of your financial history. It is a detailed record of your borrowing history, debt repayment pattern, and current credit status. This report represents a picture of your creditworthiness, which illustrates how successfully you've managed all credit accounts over time.

III. Credit Score

Now, let's talk numbers. Your credit score is a three-digit numerical summary of any information your previous credit history provides. Think of it as a summary or condensed version of the credit report, a poll around the main highlights. This score functions as a one-page summary for creditors. It outlines your creditworthiness in one short sentence.

Keeping yourself informed and monitoring the two aspects consistently, you will be better placed to take active measures to ensure your financial status is either stable or improving.

Here is why a credit report is important:

IV. Your Financial Lifeline

Your credit report is not just a piece of paper; it's the road map for your financial journey. It can form your financial future, making it possible to achieve financial goals such as buying a house, obtaining a car, or obtaining your dream job.

V. Beyond Loans and Credit

Lenders, landlords, insurance companies, and prospective employers, among others, may also inquire about your credit history to evaluate your creditworthiness.

VI. A Mirror to Your Financial Health

A credit report reflects your financial history, habits, and decisions. Its role lies in showing the course of your payment, handling debt timing duties, and answering questions about your financial responsibilities.

VII. What's in Your Credit Report?

Now that you know the significance of your credit report in your financial path, it is time to understand precisely what these important documents contain. Imagine your credit report as a meticulous map that outlines the bends and turns of your financial past to lenders. However, what underlying facts and cues does this symbolized map disclose? Let's discover **what is stored in your credit report,** expand on it, and discuss how these elements determine your credit history.

VIII. Personal Information

Your credit report starts with personal information to help know you better, like your name, gender, date of birth, driver's license number, employer info, and current and past addresses.

IX. Credit Rating

Your credit rating, categorized as low, fair, good, very good, or excellent, is frequently used to summarize your credit borrowing capability. However, some reports may display your real credit score and help lenders determine your overall financial abilities and stability.

X. Credit Products

This list shows every credit product you have owned for the past two years, including credit cards, loans, and mortgages. It contains the credit type, the name of the credit provider, the credit limit, the account's opening and closing dates, and the joint applicants' details.

XI. Repayment History

Your repayment history for each credit product within the last two years is monitored and updated through a detailed report. It enlists which repayments should be made, when they are due, how many periods can be extended, and whether or not payments were made on the given (time)frames.

XII. Defaults on Debts

This covers non-mortgage and non-financial debts like utility bills, credit cards, loans, and other types of billing online applications. When a debt is due to be paid for $150 or more and a breach of contractual agreement for more than 60 days, this is known as a default. Depending on the type of debt - credit card or loans - defaults stay on your credit report for 5-7 years, negatively affecting credit ratings.

XIII. Credit Applications

This portion records the specifics of your credit applications, including the number of applications submitted, total credit requested or granted, and any loan guarantees you made. This information helps you determine what kind of borrower you are and to what extent your financial obligations are.

XIV. Bankruptcy and Debt Agreements:

This part of the report contains information about bankruptcy filings, debt agreements, lawsuits, or personal insolvency agreements only in your name. These things have a tremendous impact on your creditworthiness and financial record.

XV. Credit Report Requests

Finally, you will see reports from credit providers seeking access to your credit report, listed below. This represents the investor's desire to obtain credit and proves that you are actively participating in the role of a credit applicant.

Table 2: What is inluded in a credit report?

PERSONAL INFORMATION	CREDIT INFORMATION
Full Name (including any aliases)	Type of Loan (such as a mortgage or credit card)
Current and Past Home Addresses	Name of the Lender
Date of Birth	Amount of the Loan
Social Security Number (SSN)	Outstanding Balanceg
Current and Past Employers	Payment History
Current and Past Telephone Numbers	Date and amount of Next Payment

XVI. How Is Your Credit Score Calculated?

Now that you know what information is included in your credit report, it is time to understand how all this data goes into your credit score's three-digit number.

This report gives a clear picture that reflects the history of your debt, payment history, and overall financial conduct. But what kind of magic happens to make the credit score from those raw data? Let's break it:

Credit scores are calculated using a history of your past dealings with lenders — a document known as your credit record. This record holds details about the kinds of accounts you've set up with lenders, the money you've borrowed or the credit limits you're entitled to, your account balances, and how you've managed payments over time.

All that data and information is collected and weighted to result in your creditworthiness rating, which ranges, for example, from 300 to

850 points. The higher your scores are, the more likely you are to repay what you owe and subsequently get lower interest rates. There are two main credit score formulas: FICO® and VantageScore®. They use the same categories of credit score data, but they differ in how the data is weighted on the credit report.

1. **FICO Score Breakdown:** FICO, or Fair Isaac Corporation, is the ultimate credit scoring authority. It uses a formula that considers several things in your credit report to determine your credit score. Here's a glimpse into the FICO scoring breakdown:

Payment History (35%): This section shows your history of paying bills, with the best results when all bills are paid on time and the worst when payments are late. This makes up 35% of your score.

Amounts Owed (30%): FICO examines your debt in detail, evaluating metrics like your credit card balances and the percentage of available credit used.

Length of Credit History (15%): Credit age is also important, and the longer the history, the better. Holding accounts open over a long period can positively affect your credit. This factor makes up 15% of your score.

Credit Mix (10%): FICO applauds the use of diverse credit lines, rewards responsible credit card usage, encourages the management of different types of credit accounts, and contributes 10% to your credit score.

New Credit (10%): Opening multiple accounts in a short period puts you at risk of attracting the attention of FICO, as your behavior could be considered a red flag of financial instability. This is 10% of your score.

Table 3: How is your credit score calculated?

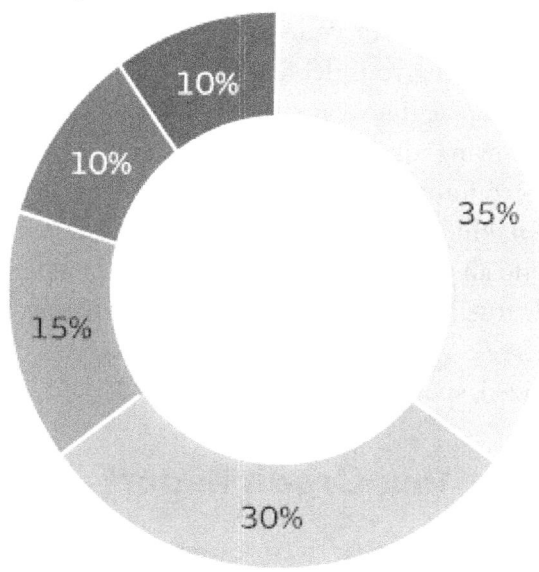

35% Payment history
30% Amount owed
15% Length of credit history
10% Credit mix
10% New credit

2. **VantageScore 4.0 Breakdown:** Although FICO remains the undefeated leader here, VantageScore has provided the market with a new vision for credit assessment. Here's a glimpse into the VantageScore 4.0 scoring breakdown:

Payment History (41%): Since their inception, FICO and VantageScore have reflected the same credit score principles by placing great emphasis on your payment record and demonstrating their belief that this is the backbone of creditworthiness.

Depth of Credit (20%): VantageScore considers not only the durability but also the complexity of credit accounts, emphasizing that credit is comprised of diverse types of loans.

Credit Utilization (20%): This shows the number of credits you're using proportionate to your credit limit, thereby exposing your competency in managing your debt.

Recent Credit (11%): The Vantage Score also consistently monitors your recent borrowing dynamics. Multiple new credit accounts can signal potential economic distress.

Balances (6%): High balances are definitely a problem in this regard, and you should do all you can to pay off your debt or at least reduce your balances. This is true even if you make all the payments on time.

Available Credit (2%): VantageScore considers credit capacity currently unutilized, spotlighting your financial stability.

XVI. Building Your Credit Report

Now that you know what factors impact your credit score, you need to take a proactive approach to building a strong credit report. A well-written credit report is like building a solid foundation for your financial future. I will be there to take you through the process from the beginning. We will discuss the various credit report-building techniques that help gain the trust of money lenders, which opens more doors of opportunity.

1. **Get a Credit Card:** You can start this run by getting a credit card. But be careful—not all credit cards are created equal. Avoid applying for cards with annual fees and interest rates beyond your capacity to pay.

Here are some noteworthy options to explore:

   i. **Secured Credit Cards:** Perfect for newcomers to the credit scene or those rebuilding their credit, secured credit cards require an upfront, refundable security deposit.

   ii. **Student Credit Cards:** Designed for college students, these typically come with rewards programs and no annual fees.

   iii. **Retail Credit Cards:** Though more accessible, you should still note their high interest rates and limitations in terms of usage.

Be aware that there is a line between using and abusing a credit card. Always remember that you can spend as much as you can afford to pay off every month.

2. **Becoming an Authorized User:** When you can't get a credit card of your own, you can become an authorized user on someone else's credit account, which is like being a passenger on somebody else's credit train. This provides the opportunity to piggyback on their credit history—but be careful! Your habits will have a direct effect on not only your credit rating but theirs as well.

3. **Use the Power of Rent and Utility Payments:** Do you know that besides the common debt repayments that go into your credit profile, rental and utility payments could also be the secret credit weapon that makes a difference in your credit history? Others do so by sending such services to the credit bureaus, where they may actually improve one's credit score. One possible solution is to enroll in rent reporting services.

4. **Find A Co-Signer:** A co-signer – maybe your parent or sibling with an excellent credit history – is what you will need to gain financial independence.

5. **Establish Good Credit Practices:** Building an excellent credit record requires not only tricks but also a steadily growing habit of financial responsibility. Strive to make on-time payments, maintain low credit utilization, spread out applications, and observe your credit state.

6. **Carefully Monitor Your Credit Scores and Reports:** Lastly, do not forget to continue tracking your credit scores and reports as you take off on your credit-building journey. Frequent checking lets you review your progress, pinpoint weaknesses, and exclude risks of missteps before they ruin your financial position.

With these savvy strategies, building your credit report like a strong fortress is easy. Thus, roll up your sleeves and set yourself on a mission to build an exceptional credit report.

XVII. Repairing Your Credit Score

Finally, the strategies for building a solid credit report are covered. Now, it is time to consider the strategies for credit repair! Think of it like doing a complete credit score makeover, going from dull to fabulous. Much like you fix your favorite gaming console or update your social media profile now and then, repairing your credit is basically playing smart to boost it and open new financial doors for you.

Now, picture your credit score like a report card for financial health. On the FICO® scale, which lists the range of 300-850, a bad credit score is interpreted as anything below 670. It's similar to getting a zero in a finance class! More specifically, scores between 300 and 579 are considered poor, but the range from 580 to 669 is fair.

Let's move to VantageScore® — another credit score model lending institutions use. Consequently, it works at intervals of 300 to 850, but the definition varies. For example, a VantageScore between 300 and 499 is described as very poor, 500 and 600 as poor, and 601 and 660 as fair. A bad credit score is like an obstacle to financial progress.

A bad score is like a dark cloud hanging over your financial future, making everything more complicated.

But worry not, as I am going to give you **some incredible and life-saving hacks to repair your bad credit score:**

1. **Review Your Credit Reports:** Keeping your credit reports in check by periodically reviewing them for errors and inaccuracies, such as your personal details being used for fraud, is a wise decision. This will assist you in resolving any misinformation you come across, which in turn will help to ensure that your credit report contains only accurate information.
2. **Reduce Credit Card Debt:** Lowering your credit card debt-to-credit ratio is one way to build your credit score—it helps to improve the utilization ratio. You should make extra efforts to maintain a very low debt-to-credit ratio, i.e., below 30%, to contribute positively to your credit score.
3. **Obtain a Credit Card:** Credit cards are a great tool that may boost your credit score if used properly. If you still don't have one,

obtaining a credit card could be the appropriate move to start building your credit history.
4. **Manage Your Debt:** Paying off existing debt is critical to lowering the debt-to-income ratio. I recommend trying some debt repayment methods, like a balance transfer or consolidation, since it is hard to repay a debt alone.
5. **Monitor Your Credit Regularly:** Lastly, remember to stay updated on the latest developments in your credit score and report, which you should regularly check. Utilize platforms like Creditwise to monitor your credit score without draining it and experience the impact of diverse financial moves.

These techniques will help you stay in control of your credit and improve your credit score in time.

Also, fasten your seatbelts because, in the next chapter, you will be on your journey of understanding investments. From discussing important considerations when investing to helping you explore investment vehicles and ways to invest in education, career, and the stock market, I will keep you updated with every means possible to be an incredible investor!

KEY TAKEAWAYS

- A credit report is an account of your financial history over a period that describes all the credit accounts, the payment status, and your debt.
- Credit reports are a crucial factor that lenders consider when evaluating an individual's ability to repay borrowed money and consequently approve them for loans, credit cards, or other financial products.
- Credit reports play an essential role in your finances by determining whether you will be approved for a loan, get a competitive interest rate on your loan, be successful with rental applications, get better insurance rates, and be able to hold down a job.

- Credit history is a required component of the financial marketplace, which is extremely important for preferred terms and market operating conditions.
- The most common information you will find in a credit report includes your personal data, credit account details (number, names of creditors, payment history, credit inquiries, and public records such as bankruptcies and liens), and credit inquiries.
- Each bureau's credit report will be different because each bureau does its own report. That's why it is crucial to review each report for accuracy through the three major bureaus (Equifax, Experian, and TransUnion).
- Credit scores like FICO® Score or VantageScore® are used to calculate a person's creditworthiness using the information presented in their credit report.
- A successful credit history is developed by adhering to timely payments, keeping credit line utilization low, operating many credit accounts, and restraining yourself from too many credit inquiries.
- One way to improve your credit score is to focus on paying down debt, making timely payments, avoiding new credit inquiries, and considering credit-enhancing options, such as Experian Boost

Teen Credit Report Template:

Name: [Your Name]
Date of Birth: [Your Date of Birth]
Social Security Number: [Your SSN]
Address: [Your Address]

Credit Summary:
Credit Score: [Your Credit Score]
Credit Grade: [Grade Assigned Based on Score]
Credit Status: [Status of Credit Report - Good, Fair, Poor, etc.]

Credit Accounts:
1. Credit Card Accounts:
- Card 1: [Credit Card Issuer, Account Number, Balance, Payment Status]
- Card 2: [Credit Card Issuer, Account Number, Balance, Payment Status]

2. Loan Accounts:
- Loan 1: [Lender, Loan Type, Balance, Payment Status]
- Loan 2: [Lender, Loan Type, Balance, Payment Status]
3. Other Accounts:
- Account 1: [Type of Account, Account Holder, Balance, Payment Status]
- Account 2: [Type of Account, Account Holder, Balance, Payment Status]

Credit History:
- Payment History: [Summary of Payment History - On-time, Late Payments, Missed Payments]
- Credit Utilization: [Percentage of Credit Limit Used]
- Length of Credit History: [Number of Years Since Oldest Account]
- Types of Credit: [Variety of Credit Accounts - Credit Cards, Loans, etc.]
- Recent Credit Inquiries: [List of Recent Credit Inquiries]

Remarks:
- [Any additional remarks or notes about the credit report

Make a Difference with Your Review
Personal Finance for Teens

"Financial education is empowerment. It gives you the ability to shape your own destiny." Suze Orman

People who give without expectation live longer, happier lives and make more money.
So, if we've got a shot at that during our time together, darn it, I'm gonna try.
To make that happen, I have a question for you...
Would you help someone you've never met, even if you never got credit for it?

<u>Who is this person, you ask?</u> They are like you — or, at least, like you used to be — less experienced, wanting to make a difference, and needing help but not sure where to look.

<u>Our Mission?</u> To make Personal Finance Skills accessible to everyone. That's the driving force behind everything I do. And the only way we can achieve that is by reaching out to... well, everyone!

This is where <u>You</u> come in. We often judge a book by its cover (and its reviews), right? So, on behalf of a struggling teen, you've never met:

Could you do us a **Favor** by leaving a review for this book?

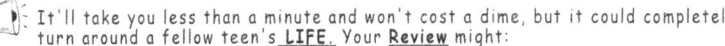

It'll take you less than a minute and won't cost a dime, but it could completely turn around a fellow teen's <u>LIFE.</u> Your <u>Review</u> might:

...Help a teen understand personal finance.
...Assist a kid in setting their financial goals.
...Support a student with ways to pay off their student loans.
...Assist them in developing personal budgets.
...Make one more dream come true.

To get that <u>**'feel good'**</u> feeling and help this person for real, all you have to do is...and it takes less than <u>60 seconds...</u>

Leave a Review!

Simply scan the <u>QR code</u> below to leave your review:

Feeling good about helping an <u>Anonymous Teen?</u> You are exactly my kind of person. <u>Welcome</u> to the <u>Club.</u> <u>You're</u> one of <u>Us.</u>

I can't wait to share with you some <u>Fantastic Communication Strategies</u> and <u>Life-Changing Skills</u> in the **Upcoming Chapters**. Trust me; you're going to love them!

 Thank you from the bottom of my heart. Now, back to our regularly scheduled programming.

Your biggest fan,
Emma Davis

CHAPTER 6

The Future Wealth

"Compound interest is the 8th wonder of the world. Those who understand it, earn it. Those who don't pay it"

-Albert Einstein

AS WE JOURNEY through personal finance, we encounter a crucial aspect that can shape our financial future: investment. Likewise, a good credit history establishes the basis for financial stability. Investment knowledge provides the key to wealth accumulation and a journey toward long-term prosperity. In the previous chapter, we ventured into the world of credit reports and scores - building a foundation for your financial well-being.

Now, think of a situation where your money acts on its own, and every dollar you spend aims at becoming bigger and bigger day by day. It is the big idea behind investing, a belief which might be now thought not certainly, yet it is the one that holds the key to financial freedom. The world of investment is vast, and there are many options for stocks and bonds, mutual funds, and savings accounts, among others, from which you can grow your wealth and secure your financial future. However, before we commence, let us first take a moment to reflect on your present understanding of investment and your level of preparation to take charge of your financial future through these questions:

Do you understand the stock market, mutual funds, bonds, and savings accounts?

Are you in a position to increase your income by increasing your efforts?

Do you have any other source of income that can enable you to achieve your desired lifestyle?

As you contemplate these questions and your answers, remember that financial literacy is a journey. Therefore, seeking advice and support is normal as you go through this process. Know that this guide will forever be your companion in this financial adventure. So, it's time to start!

I. What to Consider When Investing

At the very first step in investing, it is mandatory to weigh the important factors that play a significant role. Recognizing this will aid you in making your investment choices and keep you on track with your financial goals. Here are some important factors you must consider when investing:

1. **Understand Your Investment Goals:** The first step before you proceed to the investment world is to set the overall investment goals. What are you investing for? Whether saving for a house down payment, funding your child's college, or considering your retirement, knowing your objective will guide you to the best tactics and keep you focused on your goals.
2. **Create a Plan for Your Finances:** Establishing a financial plan specifying objectives and targets for long-term investment success is important. You can consult a financial advisor or planner to help you develop a plan that caters to your specific needs and circumstances.
3. **Understand Your Investment Timeframe:** Your investment timeframe is crucial in determining your risk tolerance and investment plan. If you are thinking of long-, short-, or medium-term goals, recognizing the time required to realize your

objectives will be the main force in making financial decisions and disciplining your approach.
4. **Understand Your Risk Tolerance:** For every investor, a tolerance of risk is different, which is the level of uncertainty you can handle concerning the potential losses while investing. Knowing your risk tolerance will be the first step toward owning an investment that fits your personality and prevents you from taking more risks than you can afford.
5. **Explore the Concepts of Diversification and Asset Allocation:** The most important term regarding this issue is asset allocation, which refers to everything you invest in different asset classes like shares, bonds, and money bases. With diversification and implementation of an approach that is close-knit to your interest, the returns will be optimized, and the risk will be minimized.

II. Investment Vehicles

Now that we have identified the factors to look for when investing, let's explore the options of investment vehicles. An investment vehicle is indeed an instrument or product that investors use to increase their money over time. These vehicles are available in various forms with different risk levels and yields.

It frequently covers stocks, bonds, and mutual funds, can involve high levels of risk, and is usually a part of a wider financial strategy.

Just as in planning a road trip, selecting the best vehicle for your investment journey is crucial. Before deciding what, you will invest in, consider where you are financially, how much risk you are ready to take, and how long you can stay invested with your savings.

Now, get ready to dive into the world of investment vehicles. Whether it's the safety of bonds or stock rev-up, there is a vehicle tailored to fit your objectives for financial growth.

Let's explore **two main types of investment vehicles: direct and indirect.**

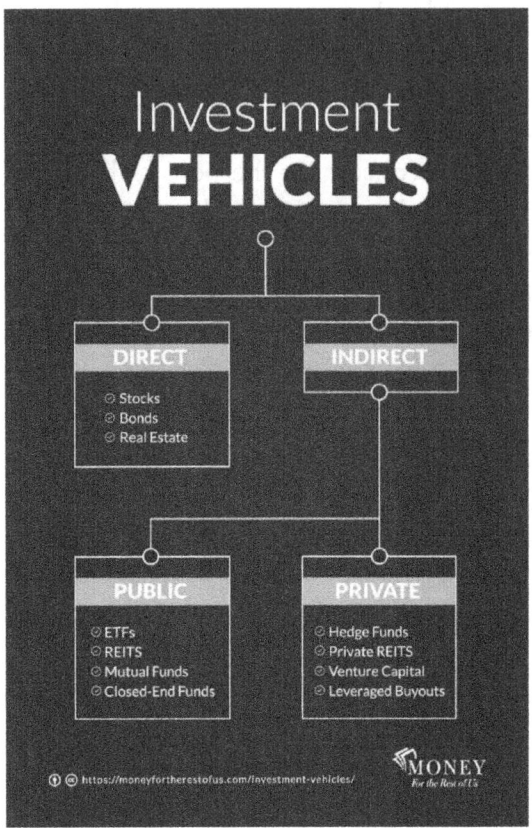

1. **Direct Investments:** Direct investments are similar to selecting some very specific destinations for your trip. You can freely decide where to go and how to get there. Here are some examples:
   - **Stocks:** By buying stocks, you are investing in ownership of a part of a company. It kind of feels like owning a small part of the business and contributing to the profit. Some companies distribute a part of their earnings to stockholders as dividends. Dividends are the payments for those who own stocks.
   - **Bonds:** A bond is a form of debt that consists of an investment in a loan made by the investor to a borrower. The regular bond will be emitted, and it may belong either to a corporation or a government agency.

- **Real Estate:** By buying real estate assets or engaging in the market through real estate, you profit from the sector and the property market. Real estate can offer a wide variety of investment opportunities to stimulate growth.
2. **Indirect Investments:** Indirect investments are similar to hiring an expert who directs you toward a good investment space. Let's break them down into pooled investment vehicles and REITs (Real Estate Investment Trusts).

    a) Pooled Investment Vehicles: They are the investment funds managed by the experts who select and monitor investments on behalf of the investors. Here are the main types.
    - **Mutual Funds:** Imagine mutual funds as baskets of shares and bonds, sometimes comprising only stocks or bonds or a combination of both. These are overseen by professionals whose goal is to increase the value of your assets over time.
    - **Exchange-Traded Funds (ETFs):** ETFs are like mutual funds, but the biggest difference is that they can be traded on stock exchanges like individual stocks. They monitor individual indexes or specific sectors and charge lower fees than mutual funds.

    b) Real Estate Investment Trusts (REITs): REIT offers a situation where, rather than buying properties, you are involved in real estate investment. They function similarly to stocks, but you own shares in real estate rather than in a company. Here's what you need to know:
    - **Equity REITs:** These strategies revolve around buying and managing various real estate types, like apartments, malls, and office buildings.
    - **Mortgage REITs:** Rather than owning properties, mortgage REITs offer loans secured by real estate.
    - **Hybrid REITs:** They are a hybrid of both equity and mortgage REITs, blending the ownership of the property and the mortgage lending.

Difference Between Direct and Indirect Investment:

DIRECT INVESTMENT	INDIRECT INVESTMENT
Specific assets or securities	Own direct investments
Lower fees	Higher fees
No portfolio manager	The portfolio manager selects investments
Complete control	Own investment vehicle, not underlying holdings
Both public and private	Both public and private
Examples include stocks and bonds	Examples include mutual funds, EFTs, and REITs

Now that you've had a chance to examine the various types of investment vehicles, you might be curious about which is the best fit for you. Not to worry, though! This guide has covered everything and will help you find the answer to that question.

Thus, your query about choosing the best investment vehicles involves goals, risk tolerance, and timeframe. Let's break it down:

III. Long-Term Goals

If you target goals such as retirement or your kids' college funds (10+ years away), direct your attention to investments with growth potential. As retirement passes, target date funds or a mix of ETFs and cheap funds can be used to buy a diversified portfolio. On your journey toward your goal, think of transitioning into a mix of ETFs and mutual fund bonds that will assist you in cutting down risk.

IV. Short-Term Goals

If you set aside money for short-term expenses such as buying a home one to two years from now, do not direct it into assets that will change their cost. If your time frame is within 3 to 5 years, choose short-term, high-quality bonds.

You will make informed choices when deciding which vehicle to invest in because you will optimize your investments according to your specific objectives and timeline. This will help you reach your set financial goals.

V. Investing in Your Education and Career

Congratulations on your commitment to building a strong financial foundation by acquiring knowledge on investment vehicles!

In the same way, you select the right investment vehicles to grow your wealth. Investing in education and career offers many benefits, including personal growth, professional advancement, and financial stability.

In this part, we will consider why investing in education for your future is so important, how it opens doors to limitless potential, what it is all worth in terms of effort and time spent on it, and, most importantly, the ways to invest in a career in education.

1. **Higher Salaries and Career Growth Opportunities:** Investment in education helps you earn higher by imparting a deeper understanding of how to be an expert in your desired field. Positions with higher responsibilities also require an educational background to earn decent pay and salary.
2. **Networking Opportunities:** Enhancing networking skills will open doors for more job options, industry information, and career enhancement. Connecting in the college network enables easy access to internships, workshops, and seminars, leading to credibility for future work opportunities.
3. **Cultivation of Work Ethics:** Individuals have the power to shape and improve their future by making informed, empowered decisions regarding their health.

4. **Personal Development and Problem-Solving Skills:** Education plays a critical role in shaping one's personality and self-improvement by making them more adaptive communicators and decision-makers. Gaining knowledge gives individuals the capacity to be good communicators, decision-makers, and problem-solvers.
5. **Unleashing Potential and Talent Identification:** Education allows one to identify and specialize in what they are skilled at through the use of degrees and training programs. The knowledge that learning offers helps to be specific about one's abilities.

Now, without further ado, let's explore the ways to invest in education and career:

1. **Enroll in Relevant Courses:** First of all, educational expenditure concerns enrolling in courses in the education establishment that are aligned to the field and job prospects. Whether these are through traditional institutions or e-courses, selecting courses according to market requirements is one step toward obtaining the qualifications and credentials that employers will need.
2. **Pursue Continuous Learning Opportunities:** Education is not restricted to formal courses but will contribute to continuous learning environments such as workshops, seminars, and certifications. Professional development through educational training that remains up to date with industry trends and current technologies will ensure job relevance and the dynamism of the markets.
3. **Seek Mentorship and Networking:** Mentorship and networking are two key tools that should be used for career development and growth. Mentors provide mentorship, advice, and encouragement as well as, if not more importantly, the process of determining how to meet career obstacles and take advantage of them
4. **Utilize Online Learning Platforms:** Online education platforms present efficient and convenient opportunities to develop new skills and absorb knowledge. These tools provide the specter of independent learning, helping people learn at their own pace and balance education with other obligations.

5. **Engage in Career Counseling and Development Services:** Vocational and educational counseling and career development facilities offer students individualized advice and support to make wise decisions concerning their lives at work and strive to achieve their professional goals.

Invest in Yourself!

While financial investments are crucial for building wealth, investing in yourself is equally important. Whether it's acquiring new skills, pursuing education, or maintaining physical and mental well-being, self-investment lays the foundation for long-term success and happiness. After all, you are your most valuable asset!

VI. Investing in the Stock Market

In the course of financial literacy and investment discoveries, stock market realization comes as an important stop on the road. Like investing in education and work, stock investment opens doors to personal and career achievements, wealth accumulation, and financial stability.

The stock market, also known as the stock exchange, is like a dynamic marketplace where publicly traded company shares are traded. In truth, just like taking courses related to your field of study or getting some educational opportunities, youth aspire to invest in businesses to earn more money and have more financial security in the future.

Let's explore **some of the benefits of investing in the stock market:**
1. **Wealth Accumulation:** The stock market opens the door for wealth accumulation via capital growth and dividends as investors buy stock shares of listed companies. They prove to be part owners as the profitability and growth of the company reflect on the stock share growth.

2. **Portfolio Diversification:** Diversifying the investment portfolio is the key to mitigating risk and getting maximum returns. The stock market presents several options for individual investors across different industries, sectors, and geographical areas, resulting in them choosing funds that reduce the effect of volatility in the market.
3. **Passive Income Generation:** Investing in stocks that pay dividends helps you glean income continuously. Companies that measure the flow of funds to the investors as a portion of their profits and pay it as dividends give those investors regular income, which prevents them from stabilizing their lives or not having any source of income during their retirement.

In short, investing in stocks gives you a chance to enjoy profits that can be higher than with other investment options, as well as other valuable benefits.

Here's a simplified breakdown of the steps to get started on your investment journey:
1. **Choose Your Investment Approach:** Decide how you will manage your money based on your knowledge, time availability, and investment style. You can choose to work with a human investment professional for a hands-off approach, a robo-advisor for automated management, or self-managed investing for greater control.
2. **Open an Investment Account:** A primary consideration is the type of account that matches your investment objectives. An individual investor selects accounts managed by financial advisers, robo-advisers, or online brokers. Research various companies rated to be the best and compare them to find the best dealership that will properly meet your needs and is compatible with other providers.
3. **Decide on Your Investment Strategy:** An advisor can help you design a portfolio adjusted to your risk profile and long-term financial goals. However, you can choose your shares and funds based on your research.

4. **Assess Your Risk Tolerance:** Delineate your risk tolerance, considering factors like the time in view, financial position, and investment objectives. Try to ascertain whether your attitude is able to withstand the turbulence of stock price fluctuations and possible losses.
5. **Monitor and Manage Your Investments:** Keep showing a cheque of your investment performance and routinely examine your portfolio to ensure it suits your goals. Watch out for the fees related to portfolio management, which will cut your overall returns.

By implementing these actions and keeping abreast of the market dynamics, you will trade stocks with certainty and gradually achieve your financial goal of being a forerunner.

The next chapter of this guide aims to assist you in making wise investment decisions by covering investment risks and returns. It will include subjects like determining your risk appetite, assessing your risk tolerance, diversifying your investments, assigning assets, and insuring your investment risks through insurance.

KEY TAKEAWAYS

- Consider your financial goals, risk level, and investment horizon.
- Know about various investment options that one can try, e.g., stocks, bonds, and real estate.
- Diversify your portfolio to distribute the risk.
- Maintain up-to-date information about the direction of the market and economic showings.
- Decide what type of investments you should choose, making sure you consider your goals and risk tolerance.
- Alternatives are stocks, bonds, mutual funds, ETFs, and real estate.
- Undertake the research, find the risks associated with every stock, and assess the anticipated returns.
- Consider the allocation across different asset classes to achieve a balanced portfolio.
- Education is a strategic capital investment that brings with it the ability to secure better jobs, higher incomes, and personal growth.
- Education brings out the heart of work ethics and the free energy of potential and builds on self-confidence and independence.
- Benefits include job security, freedom of thinking, and fulfillment of personal purposes.
- Choose a financial strategy that most coincides with your ability and the time that you have available.
- Choose the investment account that suits your needs, either self-directed or robo-advisory. You may also opt for a human advisor.
- Understand the stock market functions, such as price transparency, liquidity, and how prices are established. (Price discovery is one of the functions.)
- Use major financial advice, including setting investment targets, risk tolerance study, and professional advice.
- Be patient, set limits, and seek experts' help for successful stock market investments.

Exercise 6.1

Investment Adventure Board Game:

1. Game Components:

Game board: Create a colorful and engaging board with spaces representing different investment options, milestones, and challenges.

Player tokens: Use themed tokens like dollar signs, stock symbols, or briefcases for players to move around the board.

Investment cards: Design cards that present various investment scenarios, risks, and opportunities.

Challenge cards: Include cards that present unexpected events or financial challenges for players to navigate.

- *Rulebook:* Provide clear instructions and rules for playing the game.

2. Gameplay:

Players start with a set amount of virtual money or assets.

Each player takes turns rolling a dice and moving their token around the board.

Landing on different spaces triggers actions, such as investing in stocks, bonds, or real estate, encountering financial challenges, or achieving investment milestones.

Players make decisions based on the information presented on the cards and their own investment strategy.

The goal is to accumulate the highest net worth by the end of the game.

3. Learning Objectives:

Understanding different investment options and their risks and returns.

Learning about market trends, economic indicators, and the importance of diversification.

4. Discussion Points:

After completing the game, players discuss strategies, successes, and failures during the game.

Players discuss how the game reflects real-life investment scenarios and the importance of careful planning and risk management.

CHAPTER 7

Exploring the Risk Factor

A relevant quote at the beginning: "Risk comes from not knowing what you are doing."

-Warren Buffett

THE LAST CHAPTER about personal finance for teenagers showed us the investment side - the world of stocks, bonds, and career advancements. Before we get into the realm of investment risks and returns, let me ask you a couple of questions:
1. Do you have any savings or income-generating investments?
2. Do you have insurance to cushion you from any unforeseen catastrophes?

Now, imagine this: You have put your savings into the stock market and are looking forward to prospects with a positive mindset. Things come crashing down in an instant, and you experience huge losses on the house. You might have, for instance, already gotten the job of your dreams and might be all geared up with spare cash to pursue an education to progress your career, and in the process, you might have to update your plans one day with unexpected emergencies.

I. Understanding Your Risk Profile

A risk profile is a blueprint for your financial adventure – it's a treasure map that shows you the right way through the twists and turns of investing. However, what are risk profiles, and why are they so critical to you as a teenager exploring money management?

Simply put, a risk profile is a jargon term used to describe your level of comfort with risk when investing your money.

Finally, let's go into more detail. Risk tolerance isn't something that you only have to do with how much risk you are ready to take up – it's also about how much risk you can manage to handle based on your financial condition.

Hence, what is the procedure to determine if you are a high- or low-risk taker? This is similar to solving a puzzle. You need to consider the time frame in which you would prefer to invest, your financial goals, and how volatile you are with stock market fluctuations. Do you tend to crave an adventure and are fully up for the risky ride of stock market movement? Or would you rather have the guaranteed returns of the low-risk and secure market to avoid the risks?

The truth is, you might have higher tendencies for risks than you can bear yourself.

Let's delve into the pivotal components that constitute a risk profile:

1. **Risk Tolerance:** A key element of your risk profile is your risk tolerance, which measures your capacity to handle market fluctuations without making emotionally reactive decisions. It does this because it measures how likely you are to handle the tumultuous profit shifts.

2. **Risk Appetite:** Risk tolerance is one measure of the market, but risk appetite is a more subjective personal measure of the extent to which you are willing to take risks to achieve bigger financial gains. It closely reflects your attitude toward earning and spending and then begins to mature with your growth and experiences in life.

Although separate and independent by nature, risk tolerance and risk appetite weave into the complex texture of your risk profile. Consequently, a delicate balance between these elements would determine your direction that could serve you well and that you could be at home with.

You must keep abreast of the varied risks that may await around the corner. So, considering this, let me unravel the various types of risks that demand your attention:

1. **Strategic Risks:** Strategic risks come from external factors like new high-powered competitors, technological progress that renders the product obsolete, or an abrupt change in public tastes. These intangible adversaries not only question but also undermine the strategic purpose of an organization.
2. **Operational Risks:** Visualize the complex clockwork of organizational mechanisms to ensure that every gear fits correctly into each other for smooth operation. However, the operations function in this fragile system is permeated with risks, such as supply chain disruptions, personnel complications, equipment breakdowns, or disagreements with external partners.
3. **Financial Risks:** Financial dangers exist in another room – threatening functioning with interruptions of cash flows, liquidity problems, and untouchable interest rates. These financial storms highlight the importance of sound financial management.
4. **Compliance, Legal, and Regulatory Risks:** First, for any business idea to thrive, it is imperative to conduct thorough research and analysis. This includes surveying potential customers to determine the demand for the proposed service or product. Moreover, it is vital to evaluate the competitive landscape to identify key differences and specific factors that should be emphasized in the marketing strategy.

Now that you are well acquainted with the significance, elements, and types of risk profiles, you can move on to the procedures of forming a risk profile. Here is how you can construct your risk profile:

1. **Define Your Risk Appetite:** Commence by identifying your risk appetite—the level of risk you can face to achieve your financial goals. Consider your tolerance for risk and your ability to accept the unknown. Investing can be as individual as we are—it's essentially about your attitude toward money.
2. **Identify the Potential Risks:** Outline the possible risks you may encounter during your journey toward financial well-being.

For instance, this could be a typical financial shock from unexpected expenses, market failure, job loss, or even unexpected emergencies.
3. **Evaluating Risk Impact and Likelihood:** Explore each risk more deeply by assessing its possible consequences and determining how often the risks can be realized. Risk ranking should be based on the severity and likelihood of the crisis, as the most probable risks are always ranked higher.
4. **Customize Your Risk Profile:** You may want to personalize your risk level or disseminate a plan that fits your conditions and financial objectives. Take into account your age, income, expenses, and long-term outlook.
5. **Create a Visual Representation of Your Risk Profile:** Develop a visualization of your risk portfolio — a simple risk map demonstrating the main risks and their scale. To reduce confusion, consider utilizing color or symbol to illustrate the risk ranking of each risk, thus making an instant understanding easier.

Knowing more about the risks you may face in the future will prepare you to deal with the changing situation of personal finance.

II. Investor's Risk Tolerance

As I told you above, understanding your risk tolerance is akin to equipping yourself with the diverse landscapes of investment.

Now comes the question: Why would risk tolerance be so important? This is because it is the key to your financial plan, determining your investments while sheltering you from the worries that usually come with market fluctuations.

In general, knowledge of your risk tolerance gives you the choice to adopt an investment strategy that suits and balances well with your desire for growth and the enjoyment of steadiness. This simply is the best recipe for financial success with your unique risk appetite.

STATISTICS

1. According to a survey conducted by Gallup in 2020, about 46% of U.S. investors described themselves as having a moderate risk tolerance, while 23% reported being conservative and 30% identified as aggressive investors.
2. A study by BlackRock in 2019 found that globally, only 55% of investors feel confident in their ability to make investment decisions. This lack of confidence may influence investors' risk tolerance levels.
3. Vanguard's "How America Invests" report revealed that younger investors tend to have a higher risk tolerance, with 79% of Millennials (born between 1981 and 1996) reporting that they are willing to take on more investment risk for potentially higher returns.
4. A survey conducted by Charles Schwab in 2021 found that 44% of investors said they had become more risk-averse since the onset of the COVID-19 pandemic, indicating a shift in risk tolerance due to external factors.

Besides that, you still have to learn **the types of risk tolerance to have a good knowledge about it**. Here are a few:

1. **Aggressive Risk Tolerance:** Aggressive investors belong to a small band of the most experienced market players who are not intimidated by taking high risks in their quest for the greatest yields. They have gotten used to evidence that leads them to the top and the bottom of the market. Usually, they carefully create investment portfolios that consist of various

assets with the potential to benefit from changes in dynamic prices.
2. **Moderate Risk Tolerance:** Moderate investors are risk-aversion and growth-oriented individuals who must always seek medium ground to invest without endangering their principal investment. They might admit some degree of risk, but they may also determine the criterion of money they can lose. Among these types of investors, balanced asset allocation, with a combination of risky and comparatively stable investments, is a popular option for them, as it allows them to experience steady and stationary growth without being subjected to high volatility.
3. **Conservative Risk Tolerance:** Conservative investors tend to take a risk-averse approach; they prefer safety over risky investments with a potential for high returns. They are risk averse and take every possible measure to avert losses, aiming at higher profit gain.

Going through these types of risk tolerance, you will be equipped with a profound understanding of risk tolerance. This will help you ace your financial journey!

III. Investment Diversification

Do you recall when we discussed risk tolerance? Investment diversification is like a safety net that securely keeps you when you take risks. Diversifying your holdings ensures you don't own all the eggs in one basket. This indicates that if one investment does not perform well, the latter may help balance things. Hence, whether you are a daring risk taker or want to be more cautious, diversification is the key to managing your investment portfolio.

An investment always means having that risk, and although diversification is one of the best ways of minimizing some of these risks,

it's very important to know and acknowledge the different types of risks associated with investments.
1. **Market Risk (Systematic Risk):** Market risk, also called systematic risk, occurs when the market and all its investments are exposed to the same risk. On the other hand, uncertainty is a factor that originates from the outside. For instance, it relates to changes in interest rates, economic conditions, wars, and natural disasters.
2. **Asset-Specific Risks:** Asset-specific or unsystematic risks are directed to a particular investment or company and may be caused by the company's business results, management decisions, or industry conditions. While diversification could significantly reduce asset-specific risks, they are impossible to fully eliminate.

Let's look into how diversification benefits you:
1. **Reducing Overall Risk:** A diversified portfolio is expected to better withstand stormy market movements, similar to a team with players who can play multiple positions. If one investment does not perform well, others can make up the shortfall and reduce losses, keeping you on the right track with your financial objectives.
2. **Stabilizing Returns:** Economic environments are very volatile, but this can be minimized by having diversified assets. When some assets move down, others move up, creating a well-balanced situation that may result in better overall performance.
3. **Maximizing Potential Return:** You may not experience the adrenaline rush of betting on a single high-performance stock through diversification, but it has a better path to long-term growth. This is a unique way of setting up your financial future based on your life's expectation of different asset returns over time.

While exploring the investing world, diversification is one of the most fundamental guidelines to help you deal with the ever-changing financial markets. Widening your portfolio so that it is also exposed to different asset classes, markets, and themes may protect its value from volatility and lead to more profit.

Adhering to these principles and being disciplined in your approach can help you construct a stable, diversified investment portfolio that will bring you closer to your long-term financial goals.

IV. Asset Allocation

As you have learned, diversification in the portfolio above is a tool that can greatly reduce risk while increasing return. Nonetheless, diversification is only a starting point. Asset allocation is the next step in creating a robust and well-balanced investment portfolio.

This section examines the key role asset allocation plays in investment and financial planning, its efficiency, and strategies for diversifying portfolios.

Asset allocation means spreading your investments across different asset classes, like stocks, bonds, and cash. It is actually about maintaining a balance in the investment portfolio used to manage risks and achieve targeted returns.

There are three major types of asset allocation. They are as follows:

1. **Equities:** Equities are shares or ownership of a company comprising common stock, preferred stock, mutual funds, and exchange-traded funds (ETFs). These investments could yield returns that surpass the inflation rate and generate dividend income. Examples of equities are growth stocks and dividend-paying stocks.
2. **Cash and Equivalents:** Cash and equivalents imply quickly accessible assets such as cash, savings accounts, money market accounts, and bank CDs. These assets have certain cash-like properties and serve as a source of comfortable access to funds, but they do not give high returns, which most assets do.
3. **Fixed Income:** Fixed-income investments involve lending money to institutions such as the government or corporations for a specific period. During this period, you will receive regular interest payments and the principal back. Examples include

corporate bonds, municipal bonds, treasury bonds, and other debt instruments.

Perhaps you would like to ask the following question: What is the optimal strategy for asset allocation?

Let me help you understand this concept!

Choosing the right asset allocation for you requires you to consider a range of factors related to your particular situation, such as your objectives, age, and risk tolerance.

1. **Asset Allocation by Goals:** First, outline where you want to be by when and then the means you will use to get there. Let short-term goals such as funding your wedding serve as your guide toward stability by investing in cash or cash equivalents to run away from the vagaries of the market.
2. **Asset Allocation by Age:** Your age and the time horizon until reaching your financial goals are critical factors in your asset allocation strategy. When the child reaches his/her senior year in college, it is advisable to decrease the level of risk to protect the funds already accumulated.
3. **Risk Tolerance and Asset Allocation:** Risk tolerance assessment is essential to the process because it denotes your tolerance for market fluctuations. Despite the risk being an intrinsic part of investing, bypassing your tolerance level may cause reckless actions during a market drop.

V. Role of Insurance in Investment Risk Management

In finance, managing risks in investment is the key to securing one's financial future. Risk management involves identifying, evaluating, and minimizing risks to protect the security, health, or life of assets at stake. It also refers to the ability to endure uncertainties with emotional and financial competence

DID YOU KNOW?

Did you know that the world's first insurance company was established in 1666 after the Great Fire of London? Nicholas Barbon founded the "Insurance Office for Houses" to provide fire insurance to homeowners, marking the beginning of the modern insurance industry.

This is how insurance is a useful tool in risk management, an umbrella that protects people against unpredictable mishaps. However, insurance should rather be seen as a risk management tool to shield future income from possible threats.

Some well-known insurance companies that you may consider:

1. Berkshire Hathaway Inc. (BRK.A, BRK.B)
2. Prudential Financial, Inc. (PRU)
3. MetLife, Inc. (MET)
4. Zurich Insurance Group AG (ZURVY)
5. Chubb Limited (CB)
6. Aflac Incorporated (AFL)
7. Progressive Corporation (PGR)

Let's delve into the significance of insurance as a tool for managing investment risks.

VI. Role of Life Insurance in Risk Management

Life insurance lets you plan even the unknown. It is a financial safety network, giving your loved one financial stability even in your absence. Here's how it reduces the risk associated with life uncertainties:

Ensuring Your Family's Future: Life insurance offers a very substantial income during death, along with the family, which has been secured by insurance.

Promoting Savings and Investments: Investing in insurance is a way to encourage savings. These policies not only provide coverage but also invest savings into different financial assets, creating wealth and lucrative gains.

VII. Role of Health Insurance in Risk Management

Health insurance is like a shield that protects people from high medical bills, which enables them to receive timely and quality healthcare. Here's how it mitigates health-related financial risks:

Providing Monetary Support: Health insurance protects against the incredible cost of highly specialized medical treatments. Policyholders can undergo surgery without worrying about money, and they can rest and heal without financial concerns.

VIII. The Role of Insurance in Promoting Stability

Encouraging Economic Stability: Insurance provides the critical function of helping people and society as a whole retain economic stability both at an individual and community level. Insurance, which covers against monetary losses, helps businesses and individuals confidently invest, develop, and create jobs.

Upholding Social Stability: Along with its economic benefits, insurance also fulfills the societal purpose of ensuring that individuals and families have money to live on when facing uncertain life challenges. Insured people are less likely to have savings depleted at critical moments due to financial hardships, as they can easily rebound from this financial blow.

Encouraging Risk Management through Prevention: Insurance firms are also involved in risk management and mitigation, which are key to the stability of the whole system. Insurers thus reduce risks by analyzing risks and installing preventive measures that minimize them and losses.

Providing Peace of Mind: The primary advantage of insurance is that it gives individuals and organizations peace of mind, providing them with financial security in the face of unpredicted disasters. This certainty helps people concentrate on their daily chores, aspire and work hard to achieve their goals, and set plans for the future without worrying about imminent financial threats.

In short, life is replete with surprises, and unforeseen unpleasant situations may bankrupt you. On top of being a safeguard, insurance is utilized to secure your family's future, provide motivation to save and invest, fulfill financial plans, keep social and economic stability, and ensure your peace of mind.

Fasten your seat belts as the next chapter of your financial journey addresses the fundamentals of taxation and fees, understanding income tax, banking and brokerage fees, capital gains tax, and minimizing your tax exposure and financial service fees!

KEY TAKEAWAYS

- Know that everyone has a different risk profile that depends on their financial objectives, individual circumstance, and risk tolerance.
- Evaluate your risk tolerance by defining your investment goals, time horizon, financial condition, and emotional capacity for risk.

- Pay attention to the fact that risk profiles may evolve with time due to life events, market conditions, or broadening financial goals.
- Grasp the notion of risk tolerance that describes how much an investor can tolerate a change in the value of his/her investments.
- Understand that risk tolerance is not static and it may vary due to age, investment experience, financial stability, and personality.
- Undertake a risk tolerance test to establish your level of comfort with various types of investment risks and tailor the investment strategy to match.
- Understand the meaning of asset allocation as the method of classification of investments in different asset classes like equities, fixed income, and cash equivalents with the consideration of investment goals and risk appetite.
- Take into account that asset allocation is one of the most important elements affecting returns from investments and an investment portfolio risk in general.
- Customize your asset allocation strategy to achieve your financial goals, requirements, and risk tolerance, and examine it regularly to rebalance it appropriately.
- The fact that insurance is an important risk management tool that protects against financial losses that may result from unforeseen events such as injuries, illnesses, natural disasters, and property damage should be acknowledged.
- Know that insurance provides financial stability and security, by which you can get coverage for a variety of risks such as life, health, property and liability.
- Add insurance to your risk management strategy in order to secure financial success and make sure that the business continues to run in spite of any unpredicted problems.

Exercise 7.1

True or False: Investment and Risk Management

1. Risk profile awareness is one of the key factors to consider before making any investment decisions.
2. Investors with a low appetite for risk are more likely to invest heavily in high-risk stocks.
3. Investment diversification is an act of putting the investment in different types of asset classes to lower the risk.
4. Through diversification, you can eradicate all types of risk from your investment portfolio.
5. Asset allocation means distributing your investments among assets like stocks, bonds, and cash.
6. Asset allocation should be based only on an individual's age and not on their financial aims.
7. Insurance is completely useless in terms of financial risk management for both individuals and companies.
8. Healthcare insurance policies serve as safety nets in case of expensive medical services.
9. They provide ample opportunity for policyholders who could otherwise be worried about the affordability of medical coverage.
10. Insurance companies do not dedicate their efforts to risk reduction and management.
11. Investing in high-risk assets means higher returns over time.

CHAPTER 8

The Government's Share

"Avoidance of taxes is the only intellectual pursuit that still carries any reward."
                                              -John Maynard Keynes

I WOULD UNDERSTAND IF the last chapter overwhelmed you. It was jam-packed with a lot of content, but let me tell you, all of it was key information. Additionally, I know you may be rushing to finish your financial journey, but please do not hurry! Great things take time, and I have you covered every step of the way. Therefore, please don't be pressured and take your time to comprehend all the topics we've discussed till now. You got this!

So, for now, breathe deeply and be calm as we proceed with this journey!

John Maynard Keynes, a British economist, and philosopher, helped to transform what many thought to be unchangeable and move on to new ideas regarding macroeconomics and the economic policies of many nations. His quote above mentions the word 'avoidance.' What does this mean to you, and how has that notion evolved from the beginning?

This statement demonstrates that the concept of tax avoidance has evolved significantly over time. For a long time, tax avoidance has been linked to immoral or sometimes even illegal behavior when fulfilling one's tax obligations. Nevertheless, as tax knowledge has evolved, so has the attitude toward tax avoidance.

In personal finance, tax avoidance refers to deducting a legal approach to decrease one's or a company's tax burden.

This chapter delves into the complexities of tax avoidance and how to formulate various tactics to lower your tax liability.

However, tax avoidance isn't just about enhancing your savings — it's about financial independence. Together, we will continue on this expedition to discover several taxation secrets and how you can tap into your power as an informed consumer to negotiate the tax frontiers in knowledge.

But before you submerge yourself in taxes and fees, take a moment to ponder your financial path.

How much have you paid in account maintenance and banking transaction fees over the last year?

Do you know the different fees associated with your preferred investment vehicle?

This set of self-evaluation questions is only a starting point for a vast area of taxation and fees that we will explore further. Alright, I believe now, without a doubt, it's time we started.

I. Understanding Income Tax

Imagine you've just earned your first paycheck from working part-time and are thrilled to have some money due to your effort. While you are determining how to handle it, something new arises—an income tax payment. Yes, it's the unavoidable part of being a responsible citizen, but you can avoid overpaying the tax by understanding how it works!

Income tax is a yearly government fee based on your profit over a given year. Whether you're working a part-time job or operating an online venture, you are very likely to be taxed if you earn income.

Here's how it works: Remember to file your tax return once a year containing your whole income and the deductions that can be subtracted from your overall salary. In addition to the wage and the tax statement, the W-2 form from your employer will also disclose how much money you received and the amounts deducted from your paychecks each month as tax withholdings.

Nevertheless, you are not required to pay a uniform tax rate on all your income. The tax bracket is "progressive," which forces every income level to be taxed at different rates. Likewise, the lower part of your earned income can be taxed at a lower rate, and what exceeds the set limit can be taxed at a higher rate.

You must learn about income tax workings and how they impact your finances.

Let's start with the types of income tax:

1. **Individual Income Tax:** Personal income tax, or individual income tax, is the amount you owe based on the income you earn through wages, salaries, and other sources. This sales tax is usually directly paid by your state of residence. The Internal Revenue Service (IRS) provides different allowances and credits, which let taxpayers lower their taxable income and negate the resultant tax burden. Deductions decrease the income taxed, while credits reduce the amount of money owed in tax. For instance, if your earned income was $100,000 and you qualified for $20,000 in deductions, your taxable income would be $80,000. Also, if you owe $20,000 in taxes and are eligible for $4,500 in credits, your tax debt would be reduced to $15,500.

2. **Business Income Tax:** Companies are taxed on the income from their business operations via corporate income tax. This applies to large and burgeoning corporate projects, partnerships, individual entrepreneurs, and small businesses. The type of business structure determines who receives the income to be reported, either by the corporation, owners, or shareholders.

3. **State and Local Income Tax:** Most states in the U.S. impose federal income taxes and individual income taxes. However, eight states—Alaska, Florida, Nevada, South Dakota, Tennessee, Texas, Washington, and Wyoming—do not tax their residents at the personal income level. New Hampshire also does not tax income; it does so for dividend and interest income at a 5% rate. By 2024, this will increase the number of states without income taxes to nine.

Life in an income-tax-free state does not always mean lower cumulative taxes. These states will, in turn, make up for the lost income by implementing other forms of revenue or by lessening the services provided.

DID YOU KNOW?

Did you know that the concept of income tax has been around for centuries? The first recorded instance of income tax dates back to ancient Egypt, where workers were required to pay a portion of their earnings in taxes to the Pharaoh.

Here are **the Income Tax rates in the US:**

Income tax band	Taxable Income	Tax rate
Standard Deduction	$0 - $12,550	0%- No income tax payable
10% Bracket	$12,551 - $50,000	10%
12% Bracket	$50,001 - $80,250	12%
22% Bracket	$80,251 - $171,050	22%
24% Bracket	$171,051 - $326,600	24%
32% Bracket	$326,601 - $414,700	32%
35% Bracket	$414,701 - $622,050	35%
37% Bracket	Over $622,050	37%

Let me simplify it for you:

In the U.S., income taxes ensure that as you earn more, you pay a higher percentage of your income as taxes. Here's how it works:
1. **Standard Deduction:** This is that fraction of your income that is not taxable. For instance, earning $12,550 or less conveniently falls outside the taxpaying bracket; therefore, you will not pay any income tax.
2. **Tax Brackets:** When the required deduction is subtracted from your proposed income, the remaining amount is moved to several brackets, and each bracket attracts its tax rate. Here are the tax brackets for the tax year 2023:
    - Let us assume that your net income falls between $12,551 and $50,000. Under this scenario, you'll be required to forfeit a 10% income tax on the greater portion of your income.
    - The tax rate for income between $50,001 and $80,250 is 12%.
    - The income bracket that ranges from $80,251 to $171,050 falls in this bracket and is taxed at 22%.
    - Taxable ownership from $ 171,051 to $326,600 is subject to 24% taxes.
    - For income between $326,601 and $414,700, the rate is 32%.
    - Taxable income of $414,701 to $622,050 is taxed at a rate of 35%.
    - Any earnings above $622,050 are part of this bracket and are taxed at a rate of 37%. In the U.S., income tax rates are structured so that the more you earn, the higher the percentage of your income you pay in taxes.

TAX-FREE STATE BENEFITS

Tax-free state benefits are benefits that you can earn without having to pay income tax. The following are the most common state benefits that aren't taxed:
- Attendance allowance
- Bereavement support payment
- Child benefit
- Child tax credits
- Income-related employment and support allowance
- Industrial injuries benefit
- Lump-sum bereavement payments
- Maternity allowance
- Pension credit
- Personal independence payment
- Severe disablement allowance
- Credit
- War widow's pension
- Winter fuel payments and Christmas bonus
- Working tax credit
- Disability living allowance
- Guardian's allowance
- Housing benefit
- Income support

II. Banking and Brokerage Fees

Like navigating through the intricacies of income tax, understanding how to grow your money through investments involves another layer of complexity: brokerage fees. Like taxes, these charges are a vital part of investing that every teen should be acquainted with.

In essence, brokerage fees are the toll for driving along the investment highway. Whether you want to buy, sell, or consult, brokers charge fees for their services throughout the system.

These brokerage fees are categorized into two main forms, usually expressed as a fixed amount for each trade or as a percentage of the trade value. Let's break them down:
1. **Flat Brokerage Fees:** Imagine yourself at the market, and every time you buy or sell something, you will pay an annual fee – a flat rate. To follow the example, assume you have profits when trading stocks or buying and selling mutual funds and ETFs, and you are subjected to a flat fee per trade regardless of the size of the transaction. The fee neither increases nor decreases whether you buy or sell $5,000 or for flat-rate brokerage fees you can calculate the cost using a simple formula: The fee neither increases nor decreases whether you buy or sell $5,000 or for flat-rate brokerage fees you can calculate the cost using a simple formula:
Flat Brokerage Fee = Number of Trades x Agreed Flat Rate
2. **Percentage-Based Fees:** Sometimes, brokers charge a percentage of trades as fees. This is most popular among robo-advisor management fees and crypto trading commissions. Thus, the more investment you make, the higher the fee. For percentage-based brokerage fees, use this formula: *Percentage Brokerage Fee = Percentage Fee x Total Value of All Trades*

After learning about the various types of brokerage fees and understanding how they function, **it is time to explore the different types of brokerage fee services available. Please see below:**
1. **Full-Service Brokerage Fees:** Full-service brokers provide a broad range of financial services, such as estate planning and consolidated document services, and they are the most expensive. Initially, full-service brokers charged high commissions, sometimes reaching $100 per trade. Nowadays, this is the industry standard, with the typical range being from 1% to 2% of client's assets under management. In a nutshell, if you purchase 100 shares of a firm for $40 per share and your broker charges a 2% commission, they make $80, and the total cost would be $4,080.

2. **Discount Brokerage Fees:** Discount brokers provide limited services and options; hence, they charge less than full-service brokers. They charge a commission on each trade, with the commission rates ranging from less than $5 to over $30 per trade. Annual management fees would be approximately 0.5%, depending on the assets deposited.
3. **Online Brokerage Fees:** Online brokers have the lowest brokerage fees and are most suitable for online trading. They provide only a little customer support, but it is very convenient to work with trading platforms. Many online brokers no longer charge specific fees for stock share trades but may still charge options and futures trades.

Understanding the different categories of brokerage fee services allows you to select the right service for your investment needs and wants.

Also, note that a brokerage fee can affect your investment return, as shown in the table below. Consider, for example, the case of investing $20,000 in mutual funds with an average annual return of 10%. Here's how your investment would grow over different periods with and without a 1% annual management fee:

Period	Investment with No Fees	Investment with 1% Management Fee
5 Years	$40,263	$38,466
10 years	$64,844	$59,184
20 years	$168,188	$140,110
30 years	$326,600	$331,692
40 years	$1,131,481	$785,236

A 1% management fee will greatly impact your investment growth. Being aware of brokerage fees can minimize costs and maximize your earnings.

Lastly, brokerage fee handling is a main factor of investment management. By recognizing the different types of fees, from commissions to expense ratios, you can confidently make better decisions to favor your returns. Happy investing!

III. Capital Gains

Just like brokerage fees, capital gains tax is a significant factor in your financial journey, particularly concerning the investment and selling of assets. Let's get into the nuts and bolts of capital gains tax.

So, what is capital gains tax? In essence, when you sell something, you own and make a profit on it, you pay it as a tax. This "something" may be anything from stocks to real estate or valuables such as rare coins or other artwork. The government wants to have a slice of this profit, and we call it a capital gains tax. This is like sending a small portion of your earnings to the government as a "thanks" for allowing you to earn money from your investments.

Let's make this simple and break it down into easy steps so you can easily grasp how it works.

1. First, decide your starting point. This is the total cost of the asset or property you originally paid for and any additional charges you may have added along the way. It's about laying a foundation for your financial path.
2. Next, check your income. This is the cost of selling your property minus any transaction-related fees or charges.
3. And now, let's play a subtraction game. Subtract what you are selling from the amount you paid for it (your basis) to see how much you've made or lost. If the number is positive, it is a capital gain for you. If it's negative, that's a capital loss, which is bad. There is no need to panic; we will cover that as well.
4. Lastly, examine tax rates and pick the one that suits your situation better. Knowing how long you hold assets and your

overall financial situation will be advantageous because tax rates may differ. It's like having the right tool for every job at work.

Using these easy-to-follow directions, the process of calculating your capital gain taxes should appear crystal clear to you.

So, what type of investments have capital gains tax? A long list of asset classes in investments will earn a capital gain if sold for a profit. Let us explore the world of investments and learn which ones are **taxed at capital gains:**

1. **Real Estate Adventures:** Maybe your cozy home, holiday retreat, or investment property will fall under the category of real estate transactions that result in profits and will be subject to capital gains tax. While this is, on the one hand, sad, there is a silver lining! You might be eligible for the exclusion on the first $250,000 (or $500,000 if you are married!) of the profit from the sale of your primary residence so long as you fulfill the necessity for this exclusion.
2. **Stocks and Bonds Stories:** Stock trading or redeeming money bonds can also get you in the capital gains tax zone. However, do not be overwhelmed if you have recorded losses on the stock market; you may use those losses to escape taxes on your income.
3. **Mutual Fund Musings:** Mutual funds provide capital gains and dividends yearly, and you may be subject to a capital gains tax on those distributions.
4. **Digital Currency Discoveries:** In this digital age, virtual currencies like cryptocurrencies, stable coins, and non-fungible tokens (NFTs) are not immune to capital gains taxation. Therefore, if you are getting into the digital currency world, keep a record of your gains from a tax point of view.

Moreover, another crucial factor for capital gains taxes is the duration an asset has been in your possession. Let's break down the two main types of capital gains taxes: Short-term and Long-term:

1. **The Short-Term Capital Gains Tax:** The short-term capital gains tax kicks in when you sell an asset you've held for a year or less. These profits are, like a salary, taxed at the same rate as your

work income. Hence, depending on your income, you might face tax brackets as low as 10% or as high as 37%.
2. **The Long-Term Capital Gains Tax:** On the contrary, if you sell an asset you have held for over a year, you will face the long-term capital gains tax. Here's the good news: These rates are typically lower and more advantageous than short-term rates. The long-term capital gains tax rates vary from 0% to 20%, depending on how much you make and your filing status. Most people stick to the 15% rate.

Therefore, whether it is a short-term sprint or a long-term race, knowing about capital gain taxes can help you make smart financial moves and keep more money in your account.

IV. Minimizing Your Tax Exposure and Financial Services Fees

In the previous chapters, we have covered topics related to income taxes, brokerage fees, and capital gains taxes. Nevertheless, taxes can be the greatest investment opponent when you want to have money. But don't let yourself get stressed, as there are intelligent and legal ways to avoid or reduce your tax liabilities.

So, without delay, let's explore some strategies that could help you keep more of your hard-earned money and minimize your investment taxes.

1. **Buy-and-Hold Strategy:** You can avoid paying capital gains taxes by not selling your investments by choosing between a buy-and-hold strategy and a sell-to-avoid-capital-gains-tax approach. This is because taxes are only calculated on realized profits, and the longer your investments are, the more you can postpone paying taxes.
2. **Tax-favored Savings Plans for Retirees:** A traditional IRA and a Roth IRA's primary distinctions are taxing, disbursement rules, eligibility, fee penalty, and estate implications. Traditional IRAs are with tax-deductible contributions, taxed withdrawals, and required minimum distributions (RMD) starting at age 72.

While Roth IRAs have after-tax contributions, tax-free qualified distributions, no RMDs during the original owner's life span, and contribution income limits. Early withdrawals from both types may be penalized, yet Roth IRAs made penalty-free withdrawals of contributions. When it comes to estate planning, Roth IRAs come in handy thanks to being tax-free for beneficiaries, whereas traditional IRAs could be subject to tax consequences for heirs.

3. **Utilize the Capital Gains Losses to Produce Income:** Utilize the tax loss harvesting method and deduct the realized investment losses to offset taxable gains. This allows you to limit your tax liability by deducting the losses from the gains to achieve a lower net taxable gain.
4. **Consider Asset Allocation:** Maximize asset allocation to shelter the dividend and distribution income from tax. Dividend-paying assets may be allocated to tax-deferred accounts like IRAs that defer income taxes, and assets with potential gains may be held in taxable accounts. The fundamentals of Asset Allocation are discussed in Chapter 7 in detail.
5. **Extend Your Investment Timeline:** Take advantage of the lower long-term capital gains tax rate by holding investments for more than a year. Long-term capital gains are taxed at reduced rates of 0%, 15%, or 20% based on your income level. The coordination of asset sales under the specifications for long-term rates provides considerable relief on tax liabilities, especially for people in lower tax brackets.

In the upcoming chapter, you will find practical tips on growing your income and paving the way for more financial options. From part-time jobs and the gig economy to capitalizing on your skills, how to negotiate a salary, and getting into start-ups, you'll find all the information you need. Therefore, don't forget this opportunity to be equipped with invaluable knowledge for the future that will lead you to wealth. Go on reading, and fear not learning!

KEY TAKEAWAYS

- Know your tax bracket and filing status to determine your income tax liabilities.
- Review the tax-efficient investment strategies to diminish the tax liabilities on investment gains.
- Consider the tax implications of different sources of income, which include wages, dividends, and capital gains.
- Research and compare brokerage firms to find those with low commission rates and favorable fee structures.
- Consider variable components, such as account minimums, trading platforms, and customer service quality, when selecting a brokerage. You should be aware of all hidden fees and extra charges for services like account management, inactivity, or market data.
- Capital gains are profits from selling assets such as stocks, bonds, or real estate.
- Implement tax-managed investment strategies such as asset location and tax-loss harvesting to reduce tax liabilities.
- Participate in tax-favored retirement accounts, such as IRAs and 401(k)s, to lower taxable income and defer taxes on returns.

Exercise 8.1

Fun Activity: "Fee Negotiation Challenge"

Objective:

To prepare teenagers for discussion and negotiation with service providers such as banks, brokerage firms, insurance companies, or other similar-type organizations.

Materials Needed:

-Internet and/or cell phone access
-Pen and paper
-The list of fees and charges incurred by financial service suppliers.

Steps:

1. Preparation:
- List frequent fees and charges that may apply with financial service providers, e.g., banking, brokerage, and insurance.
- Find out the regular fees for these charges and check what services different providers offer.

2. Role-Play:
- Decide on the financial service provider with whom you would prefer to negotiate, either the bank or the insurance company.
- Assign yourself a role to play: the negotiating fee-charging side, which is the customer.
- Think of a situation where you have a problem with the fees levied by the provider firm and want to negotiate for better conditions.

Research:

- Research for alternative options and competitors' rates of the same services.
- Collect details about any promotional activities, discounts, or exclusive deals that other providers are running.

Strategy Development:

- Generate a negotiation strategy based on your research results.
- Make clear your expectations, such as a fee decrease, elimination of charges, or additional advantages.

Role-Play Simulation:

- Simulate a negotiation talk or interaction with the service provider.
- Employ telephone, email, or online chat to start the negotiation.
- Tactful, assertive, and confident while requesting lower fees or modified terms.

CHAPTER 9

Making It On Your Own

"Every effort you invest in developing your skills is a seed planted for future income growth."

-Ken Poirot

IMAGINE THIS: ONE sudden day, you find yourself in your room, planning for the future. You already know how to manage your money, but something is still lacking: if this is the case, you will not make the most of what you earn. No matter what, will that be for college, being your boss, or financial freedom, you will want to get additional money to fill your pocket. Hence, join me on a new journey as we discover part-time jobs, the gig economy, skills development, career advancement, and entrepreneurship. It is now the right time to take control of your income and follow the path of financial independence Reflect on your financial situation and ask yourself: Do you currently have a source of income? Knowing your present earning capacity, whether a part-time job, gig work, or income from your talents and skills, is the first step to financial empowerment.

Now, imagine your skills and abilities. Do you have any marketable skills? Whether you like coding, graphic design, or writing, your unique skills can open doors to new income opportunities. While reflecting on these questions, remember that earning more income doesn't mean solely earning some bucks

Let's move on to the main part of the chapter, where we will explore the strategies and resources available to help you meet high-income standards and actualize your goals.

I. Part-Time Jobs and the Gig Economy

The gig economy is a unique job market where individuals accept short-term contracts or concertize their work instead of traditional long-term employment. It allows workers to be flexible, setting their schedules and rates and choosing the projects that best suit their skills and interests.

This section will look into the various gigs from different fields, jobs, types, and income potentials.

Let's **explore the benefits of gig work!**
1. **Embracing Diversity:** In the gig economy, employers can leverage a highly skilled and varied workforce, increasing their chances of innovation and developing creative project solutions.
2. **Flexibility Redefined:** Gig workers have unbeatable flexibility. They can tailor their schedules and locations to achieve work-life harmony and peak productivity.
3. **Remote Revolution:** The gig economy is significantly characterized by telecommuting, the new paradigm of work, and its culture is centered on remote work and flexibility.

II. Developing and Monetizing Skills

Have you ever had an aspiration to turn your hobbies into viable businesses? Imagine you can earn money by doing what you like the most—writing, designing, teaching, making music, etc. It doesn't matter what hobby or skill you have. Are you one of those who can't wait to experience new adventures? Then I've got good news! In this guide, you'll discover the thrilling universe of skill monetization, and we'll take you through the steps of making your skills a sustainable way of earning. From designing products and rendering services that people value and like to marketing and growing your audience, I'll teach you the most important principles that will allow you to monetize your skills.

Here are some **advantages of skill monetization from close-ups:**
1. **Flexibility in Work:** Your ability to make money from your knowledge and competencies helps you control your work. Because you can decide whenever and however much you would like to work or from wherever you are, you can have as flexible a schedule as you possibly want to suit your lifestyle
2. **Personal Branding:** Through this endeavor, you can demonstrate your capabilities and spread the message you represent, leading to your being deemed an expert in your industry. Constructing the personal brand not only engages your credibility but also opens up doors for new chances and partnerships.
3. **Turning Passion into Income:** Wish you could receive money for doing what you do best. By monetizing your skills, you can change your activities of interest into profitable endeavors. Whether writing, graphic designing, or teaching, you can turn your creative quests into lucrative income sources.

Ready to jump on the track but need help with where to start? The following is a detailed strategy to help you along the way.

See, there are numerous ways to monetize your skills and expertise in today's digital age. Let's explore some practical ways to monetize your income:
1. **Freelancing:** Start freelancing; this is the first step to becoming self-employed and offering your services to clients who need them. Online platforms like Upwork, Fiverr, and Freelancer.com are among the best for this.
2. **Public Speaking:** Package sell your oratorical skills online and become a public online speaker. Represent the organization through speech deliveries, online or live webinars, and create popular podcasts or videos to convey your organizational goals and expertise to a large group.
3. **Affiliate Marketing:** Get paid for selling products or services related to your skills and expertise or your niche topic. Use

affiliate programs and generate income by getting a commission from every sale you attribute through your links on the website, blog, YouTube channel, or any other platform.
4. **Writing and Publishing:** Make the most of your writing talents by writing content for blogs, magazines, and websites and publishing your eBooks and articles.
5. **Photography and Videography:** Look into the possibility of selling your picture-creation and video-taking skills to non-professional online buyers. Upload your best works on platforms like Shutterstock, iStock, and Adobe to the market, or be ready to provide freelance photography or videography to clients who search sites like Fiverr and Upwork.
6. **YouTube Channel:** Create a YouTube channel showing others how to solve problems or perform various tasks. Make money through ads, sponsorships, affiliate marketing, and sales.

As you can see, these ways can help you monetize your skills. With a blend of creativity, passion, and marketing savvy, I bet you can start turning your skills into cash today!

Steps To Monetize Your Skills:

1. Discover Your Niche: Identify your passions, expertise, and the problems you can solve.
2. Find Clients: Showcase your work, network, and use online platforms to reach potential clients.
3. Stand Out: Develop a unique selling proposition, offer excellent service, and seek feedback

III. Negotiating Your Pay and Other Work Benefits

After showcasing your skills and landing a job offer, the next step is negotiating compensation and benefits. While salary is often the primary focus, don't overlook the value of other perks and benefits. In this section, we delve into negotiating beyond salary to ensure you get the most out of your employment agreement.

Now, let's imagine you've been approved for the job! Now you know that you've got to have it all right – it's time to ensure you get paid fairly for your abilities and experience. **Here are some tips to guide you through the salary negotiation process:**

1. **Assess Your Value:** Before negotiating, assess your value based on experience, education, and location.
2. **Research Market Rates:** Look up the average industry salaries to set realistic expectations and improve your bargaining position.
3. **Prepare Your Argument:** Describe why you deserve higher compensation commensurate with your qualifications and market value.
4. **Project Confidence:** Speak confidently and be prompt with your statements to ensure you are taken seriously without the impression of a snack.
5. **Stay Flexible:** Be ready to accept a substitute kind of payment instead of an immediate full salary if your employer can't, after all, meet what is being expected of them in terms of pay.

Also, negotiating job offers is more than just the figure you will be paid. I would like to share with you some of the salient benefits that you should insist on during the negotiation to improve your compensation deal:

1. **Professional Development Opportunities:** Ask for the opportunity to attend the development workshops and conferences in your field, which can give you certifications. This will ensure you won't be left behind due to the changing skill sets most needed in this field.

2. **Transportation Reimbursement:** Ask for it to reimburse transportation costs, whether for commuting to the workplace in the conventional sense or the context of business travel.
3. **Additional Vacation Time:** Engaging in dialogues to address the possibility of obtaining additional leaves provided that certain target accomplishments are achieved, paving the way for a better work-life balance.
4. **Remote Work Flexibility:** Try to agree upon the terms for your work to be part- or full-time so you can adjust your travel costs and tweak your office schedule accordingly.
5. **Educational Sponsorship:** Ask for employer-provided educational opportunities like workshops and courses if and when they relate to your role, so no effort should be put into becoming a non-professional.

IV. Investing In Your Career

Building upon the foundation of negotiating salary and benefits, investing in your career is essential for long-term growth and success.

Your career is not simply a regular job; it's a path of self-discovery you walk on, which you renovate along your lifelong learning process. Be the master of your fate, adopt a lifelong education, and you will suddenly see that your investments will make you achieve.

Here are **some effective strategies to enhance your professional prospects:**
1. **Achieve Higher Education:** The door to further education might be the best opening to keep up with the global job market and its demands—study for advanced degrees to take advantage of promotions and career change opportunities.
2. **Obtain Certifications:** Certifications in sectors like technology, project management, and human resources can enhance your credentials and speed up your professional advancement.

What Other Benefits Can You Negotiate?

- Vacation Time
- Personal days and sick leave
- Student loan repayment
- Travel allowances
- Job titles
- Hiring/Signing bonuses
- Professional development or training allowance
- Telecommuting

3. **Hone Cross-Cultural Communication Skills:** If you work in international positions or with multicultural teams, you should invest in language and culture classes to learn how to communicate properly and easily understand each other.
4. **Seek Guidance from Coaches and Mentors:** Find your coach, mentor, and career expert to help you find the right path.

V. Entrepreneurship For Teens

Getting started with business as a teenager is quite a journey that is sometimes thrilling and brimmed with enriching rewards. This is the perfect time to turn your passion into money, to express yourself through creativity, and to change this world for the better. Let's dive into the benefits learning how to be an entrepreneur can provide you when you are a teenager and shape your future path to success.

1. **Develop Essential Life Skills:** They provide a basis for the personal establishment of your future and make your life more relevant to different study dimensions and practices.
2. **Boost Self-Confidence:** Managing a business at a young age teaches a teen how to be confident as he or she goes through life challenges but still maintains the drive to accomplish different things in life. Walking this path of self-discovery and development grants you a sense of self-confidence that equips

you to face obstacles, make constructive decisions, and follow your plans with conviction.
3. **Expand Network:** Being an entrepreneur gives you opportunities to get to know others starting from scratch, learn from more experienced or successful people, and connect with others with expertise in the area you are interested in.

In this guide, I'll explore some cool business ideas for young entrepreneurs like you that can transform your dream into a full-fledged reality, as shown below:

1. **Social Media Marketing:** Let your social media skills take it to create customized campaigns for local businesses, through which you would also be able to develop your portfolio and help the businesses grow their online presence.
2. **Freelance Gigs:** By displaying your skills and ability to earn, you can show your possibilities in diverse professions such as website design, content writing, or graphic design with various private organizations or individuals.
3. **Selling Handmade Crafts:** Practice your ingenuity by making and selling handmade crafts on Etsy and any other online platform, and you can reach an audience from various parts of the world.
4. **Electronics Repair:** The opening of the electronic repairs market to customers could allow your business to provide services like screen replacements or laptop debugging, thus ensuring that you meet customers' needs in your community.
5. **Party Entertainment:** Be kids' favorite at parties! Make them laugh using character entertainment services.

Now that you have investigated some prospective business ideas and methods, it is time to understand how to start. Do not worry; organizations that exist to help you turn your dream into a reality are around. These organizations have got you covered:

1. **Beta Bowl:** Virtual entrepreneurship stages, walking our youth from concept to the marketplace, creating valuable skills and resume boosters.
2. **Beta Camp:** A 6-week remote camp where teens train to create fund-generating startups while following step-by-step instructions given by business experts.
3. **DECA:** Offering career development programs for new marketing, finance, and hospitality leaders through global educational programs.
4. **Future Business Leaders of America (FBLA):** Motivate students to act as responsive citizens by providing an environment for test and leadership experience in business careers.

They are your perfect companions that will help you turn your wildest entrepreneurship ideas into reality. Trust them and make the most of their support.

Get yourself ready because you are now getting closer to your financial goal. The final chapter of our guide, "Your Future Money: "Where Do We Go from Here?" will be the last but not least step to take action and guide yourself to financial fulfillment far from the frames of your later teenage time.

Hence, what are you waiting for? Go ahead and flip a page, and on we go!

KEY TAKEAWAYS

- Participate in part-time positions and gigs to build experience, learn basic skills such as time management and customer service, and earn income during college.
- Whether it is babysitting, lawn care, or freelance gigs, these roles have the advantage of flexibility and chances to learn from real life.
- Realize that you have your own skill set and talents, and learn how to make money with those.
- There are many ways you can categorize your possibilities, including tutoring, creating online content, selling handmade

crafts, and providing pet care services, all of which can bring you profit.
- You should never underestimate negotiating not just your salary but also your benefits.
- Negotiating is a great way to demonstrate your worth and ensure that your compensation package meets your abilities and needs.
- Invest in your career by seeking higher education, certifications, mentorship, and networking resources.
- Focus on entrepreneurship as one of the available options to fulfill your dreams and build your chances.
- Organizations like Beta Bowl, Beta Camp, and DECA have resources, mentors, and programs suitable for young entrepreneurs; they enable you to set up your startups, develop leadership skills, and positively change your community.

Exercise 9.1

FUN ACTIVITY: "Teen Entrepreneurship Challenge"

Rules:
- Divide yourself into small groups of 3-5 members.
- Provide each group with a brainstorming worksheet or canvas divided into three sections: "Ideas," "Market Research," and "Competitor Analysis."
- Explain the objective of the activity: to brainstorm three business ideas based on the participants' interests, skills, or passions and to conduct market research and competitor analysis for each idea.
- Set a time limit for each stage of the activity (e.g., 20 minutes for brainstorming, 15 minutes for market research, and 10 minutes for competitor analysis).
- Guide participants through the following steps:

a. *Brainstorming Ideas:*

In the "Ideas" section of the worksheet, encourage participants to generate three potential business ideas individually or as a group.

b. *Market Research:*
- In the "Market Research" section, prompt participants to research market trends, target demographics, and potential demand for each idea.
- Provide access to online resources, market reports, or demographic data to aid participants in their research.

c. *Competitor Analysis:*
- In the "Competitor Analysis" section, instruct participants to identify potential competitors for each idea.
- Encourage participants to research existing businesses or products in the same industry or niche.
- Prompt participants to analyze competitors' strengths, weaknesses, pricing strategies, and market positioning.
- After the allotted time, allow each group to present their three business ideas, along with their market research findings and competitor analysis.

- Conclude the activity by highlighting the importance of thorough research and analysis in entrepreneurship and encourage participants to further develop their most promising business ideas outside of the activity.

CHAPTER 10

Financial Independence

"Financial freedom is available to those who learn about it and work for it."

-Robert Kiyosaki

NOW THAT YOU have learned how to manage your finances, it's time to look at how much work you've done and what's next. I will now show you how selecting the right career impacts your financial landscape, help you learn some financial independence strategies, reveal ways to improve your income capacity, and prepare yourself if life throws something your way. Teenagers, you have almost made it — now it is time for you to start another adventure on a road of financial independence and wealth. Following this chapter, you'll have the knowledge and confidence to deal with any financial issues you might face on your path to a secure and bright future.

I. The Role of Your Career Choice and the Impact on Your Finances

As you delve into career choices and their profound impact on your financial future, it's crucial to ponder the age-old question: Does money significantly contribute to your career choice? In a world where the pressure of having financial security, that pressure clashes with your hobbies and things you are interested in doing. This makes the decision-making process a difficult and tricky task. Take into account that it's the first step of your career. You will discover what you love doing for a living and can always change your career path anytime.

1. **Education and Training:** Investing in education is the same as planting the seeds of success. Although committing the necessary time and resources for further education or certification is often difficult, the payoff in the long run far exceeds the initial costs. Whether completing a degree program, earning a certification, or enrolling in a vocational training course, every step you take to enhance your skills will create new and exciting opportunities.
2. **Do Your Research:** Your career choice is much more than your job; it is a means to financial wealth. Spend time exploring the salaries of different professions, taking into account market demand and the level of needed skills. This may require you to make tough decisions, but they will help you build a solid foundation for your future.
3. **Learn To Budget:** Budgeting expertise is a basic skill necessary for smart financial management. Being disciplined in budgeting helps you make educated financial choices, avoid debt, and focus on financial goals.
4. **Take Control of Your Student Debt:** Although student loans can be used to pay for your education, excessive borrowing can stay with you long. Make wise financial decisions by seeking part-time jobs during academic breaks to pay for fees.
5. **Choose the Right Place to Live:** Where you live can greatly determine what kind of career you can get and how much you can earn. Evaluate moving to areas with booming job markets and lower cost of living to maximize your salary.
6. **Acquire Professional Licenses, Training, and Certifications:** Always keep learning, no matter where you are in your career. For any area of expertise, there are professional certifications or training courses available that can qualify you for promotions and salary increases. By taking these trainings, you are also choosing to earn more.

7. **Pay Off Your Debts:** Debt acts as an obstacle to financial stability. Debt elimination provides the opportunity to create wealth and achieve financial stability.
8. **Negotiate Your Salary:** When accepting a job, negotiate your salary, setting the stage for further salary growth and career progression.

II. Financial Independence Beyond Your Teen Years

When you transition from your teenage years to adulthood, the concept of financial independence becomes more and more relevant. Although the idea may seem difficult, don't worry because you can start finding your way to financial freedom with the correct mindset and strategy. Here are some key strategies to empower you on your journey:

1. **Start Early:** Delaying financial autonomy by a year or even a couple of months means postponing the availability of future funds by a year or more. Start by building a healthy awareness of how you spend your money daily and work toward setting a part of your income for future projects.
2. **Budget Wisely:** Pursuing financial independence as a student starts with taking charge of your finances by developing a budget that matches your living expenses. Develop a good habit of keeping a record of your expenses and recognize your necessary spending.
3. **Invest in Yourself:** Commit to your education, skills, and self-improvement on a continuous basis. Seek other education alternatives, such as certifications and other skills, to increase your salary and worth.
4. **Diversify Income Streams:** Delve into the numerous ways to earn money aside from traditional employment. Take on freelancing or part-time work, or seize the opportunity to earn income by creating something from your interests and skills.

5. **Manage Debt Responsibly:** Debt accumulation is a definite menace, so manage any current debts responsibly. Be aware of credit limits when using a credit card.
6. **Seek Financial Literacy:** Being aware of the importance of personal finance, you must be knowledgeable in budgeting, debt management, and investing principles. To supplement the skills you learn, utilize various online tools, participate in workshops, or read books to help you make smart financial decisions.
7. **Set SMART Goals:** It is essential that you set clear, measurable, and attainable goals as part of your journey toward financial freedom. Be sure to break major milestones into short-term, achievable goals, and remember to show yourself some grace while you work toward the bigger picture.

Adhering to the above-mentioned steps and having a purposeful attitude toward personal finance will help you not only deal with finances but also manage them successfully.

III. Increasing Your Capacity to Earn

Are you ready to take command of your earning capacity? Leaning on what you have already achieved in your financial life and smart money management, we must move forward and look at the possibilities of making more. Knowing your possible earnings opens up the gates to financial freedom and career opportunities for the future.

Have you ever imagined how much you could earn over the limit of your current paycheck? Actual income is all about the opportunities that depend on your skills, employment history, educational qualifications, and even where you live.

With an understanding of the role of potential income and its impact on your financial future, you are now ready to explore some practical approaches to increase your income.

1. **Networking:** Networking isn't just about collecting business cards—it's about establishing real relationships that can open new possibilities. Attend industry seminars, events, or conferences to make professional contacts and grow your professional network.

Fostering connections with other professionals will help you gain information to forge your way toward a successful career.
2. **Language Proficiency:** In the globally connected world, fluency in many languages is valuable. Try learning a new language to widen your communication skills and gain a competitive advantage in various industries. Multilingualism or being bilingual can expand your career opportunities.
3. **Time Management:** Efficiency and productivity are two of the most important factors in the workplace. With enough self-discipline to do things well, meet deadlines, and produce high-quality work, achieving educational objectives becomes possible.
4. **Entrepreneurship:** The alternative of going for entrepreneurship or a side hustle is a great way of earning extra income while pursuing your passion. Whether a small business or freelancing, entrepreneurship offers wealth accumulation and autonomy opportunities.
5. **Financial Literacy:** Understanding basic personal finance and investment is a basis for income growth. Educate yourself on subjects like budgeting, saving, investment, and retirement planning to make rational financial decisions.

Enhancing your monthly income isn't just about earning more. It's about creating growth opportunities and stability in the long run.

IV. Be Ready for the Unexpected

Life is full of surprises ranging from good to bad. Although we usually expect the best, preparing for the worst is just as important. It can be from a sudden job loss, medical emergencies, or natural disasters. These unexpected events can destabilize your life and finances. In this last section, we'll discuss the necessity of being prepared for anything and how you can take certain practical steps to keep your financial wellness intact.

Here are some practical ways to safeguard your financial well-being:

1. **Take Charge of Budgeting and Debt Management:** Having a budget allows you to see your income and expenses and be ready for unexpected situations. Moreover, an emergency budget will serve as a safety net during prolonged financial hardships. With high-interest credit cards, do not forget to pay them off early and keep the mortgage and auto loan balances under 15-20% of your income.
2. **Start Saving for an Emergency Fund:** An emergency fund with 3 to 12 months of living expenses can be a safety net during unexpected events like job loss or medical bills. Set some aside in savings and the rest in a money market account for extra safety.

> **DID YOU KNOW?**
>
> According to a survey by Bankrate, only 41% of Americans have enough savings to cover a $1,000 emergency expense, highlighting the necessity of emergency funds.

3. **Prepare for Disasters:** Think about natural and man-made disasters in your area. Make sure that you are adequately insured. Moreover, keep your emergency kit handy with the necessary supplies and store important documents in a safety deposit box or in secure places.

DID YOU KNOW?

Over 50% of American workers have less than $50,000 saved for retirement, emphasizing the importance of early retirement planning.

4. **Maintain Insurance:** Health, life, home/renters, auto, and disability insurance protect you from any financial crisis. Be sure to review your coverage repeatedly to ensure you are adequately covered.
5. **Save for Retirement:** Start saving for retirement as early as possible and invest as much as possible in your retirement plan. Retirement might be earlier than you thought, so it is advisable to be ready.
6. **Setting up Estate Planning Documents:** Safeguard your estate by naming beneficiaries for retirement accounts and creating key documents such as a will, durable power of attorney, and living will.

Implementing such measures will help you be in a better position when the unexpected happens, ensuring your financial security and peace of mind.

Test Your Knowledge: Statements And Reasons

Write the appropriate reasons for the following statements:

Statement 1: Budget is the most vital part of financial management.

Statement 2: Investment in education and skills increases earning potential.

Statement 3: Establishing an emergency fund has financial security at its core.

Statement 4: Adequate coverage provides insurance against the financial crisis.

Statement 5: Networking is the key to career development.

Statement 6: Lifelong learning, constant skill acquisition, and improvement result in personal and professional development.

Statement 7: Saving for retirement guarantees future financial sufficiency.

Statement 8: A plan for emergency preparedness is necessary in unexpected cases.

KEY TAKEAWAYS

- Your career choice decides your financial condition in the long run.
- Put education and training first, research job earning capacity, and learn how to manage your budget to increase your income from the very beginning.
- Gain knowledge of budgeting, saving, investing, and debt management to eventually enjoy financial independence.
- Constantly increase your ability to earn more by spending on education and certificates, participating in professional development programs, and networking.
- Try to learn new things like languages, find a mentor, and learn how to manage your time well. It will also provide you with a high income.
- Be ready for unexpected financial matters by studying budgeting and debt management, building a rainy-day fund, and disaster planning.
- Make sure you have the right insurance coverage, save for your retirement, manage your retirement cash flow, and fill out a will and other basic estate planning documents.

CONCLUSION

NOW THAT IT is time to bid farewell, let's recap all that we learned in this guide. From understanding personal finance to setting financial goals and evaluating progress, I have tried to cover everything that will help you on your journey. We explored budgeting, guiding you to track your income and spending, create a personal budget, and stick to it. Saving culture development is also one of our major objectives, and we touched on several approaches to saving, the role of compound interest, and the influence of inflation on savings.

In addition, we also spoke about having debts and debt management, giving examples of good and bad debts and ways to balance the load of debts. Another major item was your credit score, its calculation, and the steps to build and repair it.

When discussing investments, we mentioned some common factors, such as investment vehicles and the importance of investing in your career and education. We also looked into investment risk and returns; you now understand your risk, diversification, and the role of insurance.

We also covered income tax, banking fees, and ways to stabilize tax exposure. The other was increasing income with counsel on part-time work, skills development, negotiation, and entrepreneurship.

Career choice was also crucial. We discussed financial independence, increasing earning potential, and being ready for the unexpected were all taken up. This in-depth guide taught you the skills and tools to navigate your financial road confidently.

At the end of this journey, let me remind you that the knowledge you are carrying is immense. From basic understanding to the difficult investment and taxation aspects, you have the skills to take charge of your financial future. Make your budget, save regularly, and keep debts under control. Be on top of your credit all the time, gain financial literacy, and evaluate the risks in investments. Be aware of taxes and fees, and constantly look for ways to increase your earnings. Remember to be ready for the unforeseen as you plan for the road ahead. Whether it is through being in a career you really want, having financial independence, or building a strong savings cushion, being prepared for life's surprises means everything. Therefore, as you walk with determination, armed with this newly discovered knowledge, please don't stop being inquisitive, informed, and empowered. The financial path you have been walking on has just started, and with the skills you have gotten from this guide, you are on a good footing to steer through the journey ahead of you.

Now, take a break to consider some of the inspiring success stories that have cleared your own path to financial independence. As MrBeast, JoJo Siwa, and Logan Paul demonstrate, the same is possible for each of you, with their unparalleled success due to the convergence of hard work, creativity, and strategic fiscal management.

In the same way, these amazing people were able to create their paths to success, you can also begin moving toward financial freedom. Using the principles and strategies covered here, you can become a JoJo Siwa, MrBeast, or Logan Paul yourself.

We end this guide with confidence and some personal finance knowledge and insights. It is high time to start exercising your skills. From now on, you will be a self-empowered individual who will use all the tools at your disposal to design the future you want for yourself. Therefore, take your chance, use the strategies described, and begin the journey to financial independence. The hurdles ahead will undoubtedly be extremely hard, but maintaining determination, persistence, and knowing exactly what you want will ensure your success. Hence, chin up with courage to champion your desired future.

Teens, do not meander into being without a plan; start the path to independent financial success. With perseverance in your heart and the knowledge acquired from these pages, you can commence on a path toward freedom from financial dependence.

The first steps may be to create your budget, record your spending, and regularly contribute a part of your allowance into your savings. As your confidence levels skyrocket, you can venture into different ways of making more money, such as tutoring your peers or even starting a small online business selling handmade crafts. You can start financing for your future by applying your skills and entrepreneurial mindset through the stock market or real estate investing. This is also when you will watch your savings grow, your investments prosper, and you will realize the power of money in your hands.

From a curious teenager with lofty goals to a financially wise young adult with a shining future, your path can serve as an embodiment of knowledge and ambition.

Hence, this guide has you covered, and with a pinch of belief in your abilities, the sky is the limit. Your success story is now in your own hands. Are you ready to forge ahead?

Finally, I invite you, the teenagers with whom I traveled through the guide, to come together. If you have found this book to be positive, helpful, or fun, let me know by writing a review on Amazon. Not only does your opinion guide other teens toward the book, but it also gives important information for future readers. As such, whether you choose to leave a few words yourself or simply want to demonstrate your support, we would enjoy hearing from you. I would like to thank you for accompanying me through this journey into the field of personal finance and not forgetting the importance of your potential.

Answers

Exercise 4.1.

M.C.Q'S

1. b.
2. c.
3. b.
4. c.
5. b.

Exercise 7.1

True/False

1. True
2. False
3. True
4. False
5. True
6. False
7. False
8. True
9. True
10. False
11. False

Exercise 10.1

Reasons

Reason 1: It helps you track your spending, prevents you from getting into debt, and helps you achieve financial goals and be prepared for emergencies as well.

Reason 2: Higher educational levels and specialization skills make the development of professional careers much easier, with more income, flexibility, and growth.

Reason 3: It provides assurance, avoids debt accumulation, creates opportunity, and reduces financial stress.

Reason 4: Risks are reduced, financial stability is ensured, legal requirements are adhered to, and peace of mind is gained.

Reason 5: It increases your network, provides chances for mentorship, facilitates learning, and gives you a gateway to new career opportunities.

Reason 6: Developing new knowledge and improving skills result in better job performance, higher employability, more confidence, and faster promotion.

Reason 7: It creates financial independence, secures income after retirement, gives tranquility, and enables one to enjoy life after work.

Reason 8: It minimizes disruption during crises, ensures safety and well-being, clarifies action steps, and promotes resilience in adverse situations.

Make a Difference with Your Review Personal Finance for Teens

Now you have everything you need to achieve financial success; it's time to pass on your newfound knowledge and show other readers where they can find the same help.

Simply by leaving your honest opinion of this book on Amazon, you'll show other teens where they can find the information they're looking for and pass their passion for Personal Finance Skills forward.

Thank you for your help. Personal Finance is kept alive when we pass on our knowledge – and you're helping us to do just that.

https://www.amazon.com/review/review-your-purchases/?asin=BOOKASIN\
>> Click here to leave your review on Amazon.

leave a review

ABOUT THE AUTHOR

EMMA DAVIS is a woman who wears many hats. She is a clinical social worker, a therapist, and a financial advisor, as well as the author of Effective Anger Management for Teens.

Her books are aimed at teenagers, covering a diverse range of topics, including life and coping skills, DBT techniques, finances, puberty, developing a growth mindset, and career planning. She focuses on the unique challenges faced by adolescents in their emotional and physiological development, empowering readers with a strong foundation for understanding.

Emma draws on experience and knowledge from all her roles, as well as her experience as a mother, to guide young people through the difficult stage of adolescence. She runs a therapy practice and financial education agency tailored to teenagers, and has worked with a diverse range of young people facing different practical and emotional challenges. She also runs several online courses on cultivating interpersonal skills, gratitude, happiness, and joy, as well as 10 residential care facilities for adults with disabilities and mental health challenges, which also informs her work.

Emma is married with 9 children between the ages of 3 and 22. She enjoys spending time with her family, practicing jiu jitsu, and developing her skills in photography.

Helping Teens With Finances, Anger Management, Mental Health, And Future Life Planning

From
EMMA DAVIS

Available on Amazon or wherever books are sold

To learn more about helping teens with finances, anger management, mental health, and future life planning

please join my newsletter!

at www.emmadavisbooks.com

REFERENCES

7 tips for reducing your expenses. (n.d.). Truist. https://www.truist.com/money-mindset/principles/budgeting-by-values/reducing-your-expenses

Bamboo. (2023, June 8). The Psychology of Investing: How emotions affect our investment decisions. https://www.linkedin.com/pulse/psychology-investing-how-emotions-affect-our-investment-decisions

Brock, C. (2023, November 10). Asset Allocation by Age: 5 Things to Know. The Motley Fool. https://www.fool.com/retirement/strategies/asset-allocation-by-age/#:~:text=Asset%20allocation%20is%20the%20diversification

CFI Team. (2024). Risk Tolerance. Corporate Finance Institute. https://corporatefinanceinstitute.com/resources/wealth-management/risk-tolerance/

Christie, I. (n.d.). 10 Reasons to Invest in Your Career. Monster.com. https://www.monster.com/career-advice/article/10-reasons-to-invest-in-your-career

Einstein's Compound Interest - The 8th Wonder of the World. (n.d.). Www.greatestgiftapp.com. Retrieved June 17, 2024, from https://www.greatestgiftapp.com/blog/einstein-compound-interest

Expert, A. T. (n.d.). Understanding progressive, regressive, and flat taxes. TurboTax Tax Tips & Videos. https://turbotax.intuit.com/tax-tips/general/understanding-progressive-regressive-and-flat-taxes/L917X2gBs

Fidelity Smart Money. (n.d.). How is your credit score calculated-and what does it mean? | Fidelity. Www.fidelity.com. Retrieved

June 17, 2024, from https://www.fidelity.com/learning-center/smart-money/how-is-credit-score-calculated

Frankel, M. (2023, October 13). Guide to Brokerage Fees. Www.fool.com; Motley Fool. https://www.fool.com/the-ascent/buying-stocks/guide-to-brokerage-fees/

Fox, M. (2021, January 14). Want a fun way to teach your kids about money?

Ganti, A. (2024, May 17). What is a budget? Plus 10 budgeting myths holding you back. Investopedia. https://www.investopedia.com/terms/b/budget.asp

Good Debt Vs. Bad Debt. (n.d.). Schwab MoneyWise. https://www.schwabmoneywise.com/essentials/good-debt-vs-bad-debt#:~:text=Too%20much%20debt%20can%20turn,lead%20to%20an%20unsustainable%20lifestyle.

ICICI Direct. (2023, November 27). Understanding the Risk Profile: Definition, Importance, and Examples. ICICI Direct; ICICI Direct. https://www.icicidirect.com/research/equity/finace/understanding-the-risk-profile-definition-importance-and-examples#:~:text=Components%20of%20a%20Risk%20Profile&text=It%20refers%20to%20your%20ability

Kiyosaki, R. T. (2015). Rich dad poor dad. Robert Kiyosaki.

Kahn, J. R., & Pearlin, L. I. (2006). Financial Strain over the Life Course and Health among Older Adults. Journal of Health and Social Behavior, Vol 47 (March): 17–31, 24. https://doi.org/DOI: 10.1177/002214650604700102

Matthews, M. (2023, February 1). How to Create a Budget in 7 Steps | Indeed.com. Www.indeed.com. https://www.indeed.com/career-advice/pay-salary/how-to-create-a-budget

O'Shea, A., & Lam-Balfour, T. (2023, May 17). How Asset Allocation Impacts Your Portfolio. NerdWallet. https://www.nerdwallet.com/article/investing/what-is-asset-allocation

Porter, T. J. (2023). How To Make A Monthly Budget In 5 Simple Steps. Bankrate. https://www.bankrate.com/banking/how-to-make-a-monthly-budget/

Pilcher, J. (2023, September 20). The Piggy Bank origin Story: An accidental invention. The Financial Brand.

Raisin UK. (n.d.). Income tax rates and tax brackets explained. Www.raisin.co.uk. Retrieved June 17, 2024, from https://www.raisin.co.uk/taxes/income-tax-rates/#:~:text=If%20you%20earn%20

Role of Insurance in Risk Management. (2022, April 20). Future Generali India Life Insurance. https://life.futuregenerali.in/life-insurance-made-simple/savings-investments/role-of-insurance-in-risk-management/

Six Ways to Invest in Your Career. (n.d.). Monster.com. Retrieved June 17, 2024, from https://www.monster.com/career-advice/article/6-ways-to-invest-in-your-career-hot-jobs

Stein, D. (2023, August 14). A Complete Guide to Investment Vehicles. Money for the Rest of Us . https://moneyfortherestofus.com/investment-vehicles/

Stevens, K. (n.d.). How to save money in Seoul. https://gocity.com/en/seoul/blog/how-to-save-money-in-seoul

Texas, P. F. (2021, May 29). How Do Career Choices Affect Your Income? Power Finance Texas. https://powerfinancetexas.com/blog/career-choices-that-affect-income/

Top Budgeting Tools and Software for Finance Mastery - Training for Financial Services. (2023, December 22). https://esoftskills.com/fs/budgeting-tools-and-software/

Unbiased. (2024, February). Starter guide to investing in equities. Unbiased.co.uk. https://www.unbiased.co.uk/discover/personal-finance/savings-investing/how-to-start-investing-in-stocks-and-shares

Williams, T. (2023, December 29). 10 Ways Student Debt Can Destroy Your Life. Investopedia. https://www.investopedia.com/articles/personal-finance/100515/10-ways-student-debt-can-destroy-your-life.asp

Kövecses, Z. (2010, 14 de diciembre). Anger: Its language, conceptualization, and physiology in the light of cross-cultural evidence. De Gruyter. https://www.degruyter.com/document/doi/10.1515/9783110809305.181/pdf?licenseType=restricted

von Salisch, M., & Vogelgesang, J. (2005). Regulación de la ira entre amigos: Evaluación y desarrollo desde la infancia hasta la adolescencia. Journal of Social and Personal Relationships, 22(6), 837-855.

Debaryshe, B. D., y Fryxell, D. (1998). Una perspectiva evolutiva de la ira: Family and peer contexts. Psychology in the Schools, 35(3), 205-216.

Edición - Volumen 14, julio de 2017, número 3. (s.f.). https://biblioscout.net/journal/ pm/14/3#page=30

Lehane, O. (2019, 1 de marzo). Cómo lidiar con la frustración: Un estudio de teoría fundamentada de practicantes de CVE. DOAJ (DOAJ: Directory of Open Access Journals). https:// doi.org/10.4119/ijcv-3105

Wright, S. F., Day, A., & Howells, K. (2009, 1 de septiembre). Mindfulness y el tratamiento de los problemas de ira. Aggression and Violent Behavior (impreso). https://doi. org/10.1016/j.avb.2009.06.008

Bickram, S. (2019). A Quantitative Analysis between Anger and Assertiveness Communication Styles among Online Students (Tesis doctoral, Keiser University).

Malmir, R., & Nedaee, T. (2019). La relación entre el control de la ira y la actividad física. Salud, 21(4), 284-291.

Steffen, S. L., y Fothergill, A. (2009, 1 de marzo). 9/11 Volunteerism: A pathway to personal healing and community engagement. the Social Science Journal/la Revista de Ciencias Sociales. https://doi.org/10.1016/j.soscij.2008.12.005

Sharma, M. K., Sunil, S., Roopesh, B. N., Galagali, P., Anand, N., Thakur, P. C., Singh, P., Ajith, S., & Murthy, K. D. (2020, 1 de enero). El fracaso digital: Un motivo emergente de expresión de ira entre los adolescentes. Industrial Psychiatry Journal/Revista de Psiquiatría Industrial. https://doi.org/10.4103/ipj.ipj_81_19

Wollebæk, D., Karlsen, R., Steen-Johnsen, K., & Enjolras, B. (2019). Ira, miedo y cámaras de eco: La base emocional del comportamiento en línea. Social Media+ Society, 5(2), 2056305119829859.

Almourad, M. B., Alrobai, A., Skinner, T., Hussain, M., & Ali, R. (2021, 1 de noviembre). Digital wellbeing tools through users lens. Technology in Society (Print). https:// doi.org/10.1016/j.techsoc.2021.101778

Sadagheyani, H. E., Tatari, F., Raoufian, H., Salimi, P. S., & Gazerani, A. (2021, 1 de mayo). The effect of multimedia-based education on students' anger management skill. Educación Médica (Ed. Impresa). https://doi.org/10.1016/j.edumed.2020.09.020

Kassinove, H., y Sukhodolsky, D. G. (1995). Anger disorders: Basic science and practice issues. Temas de enfermería pediátrica integral, 18(3), 173-205.

Üzar-özçetin, Y. S. (s.f.). Effects of Structured Group Counseling on Anger Management Skills of Nursing Students | Journal of Nursing Education. Journal of Nursing Education. https://journals.healio.com/doi/abs/10.3928/01484834-20170222-10

Made in the USA
Monee, IL
15 April 2025

15844376R00089